THE

Many Loves of

Marriage

THE
Many Loves
of Marriage

Thomas & Nanette
KINKADE

with LARRY LIBBY

Multnomah Publishers® *Sisters, Oregon*

THE MANY LOVES OF MARRIAGE
published by Multnomah Publishers, Inc.
© 2002 by Thomas and Nanette Kinkade
Cover artwork by Thomas Kinkade © 2002 by Thomas Kinkade,
Media Arts Group, Inc., Morgan Hill, CA
International Standard Book Number: 1-59052-149-8

Cover design by Koechel Peterson & Associates, Inc.
Interior typeset by Katherine Lloyd, The DESK, Bend, Oregon

Unless otherwise indicated, Scripture quotations are from:
The Holy Bible, New International Version
© 1973, 1984 by International Bible Society,
used by permission of Zondervan Publishing House
Other Scripture quotations are from:
The Message
© 1993 by Eugene H. Peterson
New American Standard Bible® (NASB) © 1960, 1977, 1995
by the Lockman Foundation. Used by permission.
Revised Standard Version Bible (RSV) © 1946, 1952 by the
Division of Christian Education of the National Council of the Churches of Christ
in the United States of America
"You Are God" by Scott Underwood © 1997 Mercy/Vineyard Publishing.
All rights reserved. Used by permission.

Multnomah is a trademark of Multnomah Publishers, Inc.,
and is registered in the U.S. Patent and Trademark Office.
The colophon is a trademark of Multnomah Publishers, Inc.
Printed in the United States of America

For information:
MULTNOMAH PUBLISHERS, INC.
POST OFFICE BOX 1720
SISTERS, OREGON 97759

Library of Congress Cataloging-in-Publication Data:
Kinkade, Thomas, 1958–
    The many loves of marriage / by Thomas & Nanette Kinkade.
        p.cm.
Includes bibliographical references.
    ISBN 1-57673-953-8 (hardback)
978-1-59052-149-6 (paperback)
1. Kinkade, Thomas, 1958–   2. Painters—United States—Biography.
3. Kinkade, Nanette.   4. Painters' spouses—United States—Biography.
I. Kinkade, Nanette.   II. Title.
    ND237.K535 A2 2001
    759.13—dc21

                        2001006091

                    146646482

DEDICATION

To all those who still cherish
the dream of marriage as a place
of friendship and love.

CONTENTS

Can you
hear the whisper
of summer wind
along the
tree-lined streets?

CHAPTER ONE

Where Love Begins

Picture a classic American town of a simpler era: a white stone courthouse at its center, Main Street winding its way between awning-clad shops and offices, row upon row of quaint village lanes overspread with shade trees.

Picture following U.S. Highway 50 up from Sacramento toward Lake Tahoe, curving through towns like Shingle Springs, El Dorado, and Missouri Flat on your way into the sun-splashed foothills.

Picture a sleepy community nestled in those hills, girded with apple and pear orchards, mantled with forests of oak and pine reaching into the hazy blue of the High Sierras.

Picture Main Street itself, antique lampposts lining the sidewalks, historic buildings of brick or weathered wood on either side of the street, some dating from the rough 'n' ready Gold Rush days of the 1850s.

Picture an iron bell tower at the town's central square, an American flag rippling languidly from one of the upper crossbars.

Can you see it all on a hot June afternoon? Can you imagine a sky as clear and deep and blue as a mountain lake? Can you catch the fragrance of sun-warmed pines wafting down from the hills? Can you hear the clatter of dusty pickup trucks dropping off farm kids for an afternoon in town, or the friendly murmur of sidewalk gossip as neighbors pause to pass the time of day? Now, look up one of those side streets coming down out of the scruffy, hillside neighborhoods. Can you spot the young boy in ragged jeans, Keds sneakers, and a faded, striped Tshirt, flying down the hill on a Stingray bicycle?

That's me, Thom Kinkade.

And that's my hometown, Placerville, California.

If you had seen me on such a day, I might well have been heading into town for my summer haircut at the downtown barbershop. After ten minutes or so (it doesn't take long to administer a flattop on a boy's head if he sits still), I would emerge with newly exposed ears and a tidy crop of bristly brown hair. The barber's vain attempts to create a part in the remaining undergrowth were to no avail. This would perhaps be the last time a comb would touch my head for the next month or two.

My barber had decades of experience cutting little boys' hair. But he was also a bit of a lush, and if you got your hair trimmed in the afternoon, more than likely he would have already paid one or more visits to the Round Tent Saloon, a watering hole dating back to 1849 or so. You could never be sure what the results of your visit to the barbershop would be. But what did a bald patch or two matter? Eight-year-old boys are supremely indifferent to the quality of their haircuts. Of much greater interest was the barber's prowess as a storyteller.

This was one of those old-fashioned barbershops where two or three old men in overalls always seemed to be sitting. Loafers, we called them. They never seemed to have much of anything to do except sit in the barber chairs chewing tobacco, leafing through ancient pinup magazines, and telling yarns about recent fishing trips. The barber himself had an interesting conversational style. No matter what you were talking about, you always ended up in World War II. It wouldn't be long before he would drawl, "Well, back in the war…." And he would launch into an oft-repeated tale of brave deeds, exotic places, and the antics and camaraderie of young soldiers far from home.

The shop was a cheerful chaos, littered with candy wrappers, cigarette butts, old newspapers, and piles of hair that the barber would move around from time to time with an indifferent nudge from his broom. But the price was right—one dollar—for a haircut that would last you almost all summer.

Freshly shorn and redolent of Butch Wax, I'd step out onto the hot sidewalk and hit some of my favorite haunts before heading home. Good old Main Street! To this day, I can close my eyes and see the signs of local merchants proudly hung from awnings that provided shade along the sun-baked streets. The Bluebell Cafe, P&M Market, Raffle's Hotel, Florence's Dress

Shop, and Mac's Jumbo, the local malt shop. At the Hangman's Tree Saloon (a competitor of the Round Tent) a cowboy mannequin dangled in effigy from a noose attached to a tree limb nailed to the front facade.

At Vesuvio's Pizzeria, you could look through the front window and watch the guy in the white apron tossing pizza dough high in the air. At Blair Brothers Lumber Company, east of town, the man behind the counter would give you a free yardstick. Up the street a couple of blocks, at Chuck's Frosty, you could get a soft-serve ice cream cone for a dime.

For ten cents you could get a two-foot-long bag of popcorn.

When my friends and I were doing the rounds, we'd usually start with the Ben Franklin Five-and-Dime—a real town landmark. The old ladies who ran the place frowned and harrumphed when my buddies and I came through the door, convinced we were stealing them blind. Oh, sure. As if we were tempted by all the thimbles, thread, dress patterns, and sewing implements they had on display! What we came for was their popcorn machine. For ten cents you could get a two-foot-long bag of popcorn—every bit as fresh and tasty as you'd get at the Empire Theater next door for twice the price.

From there, we'd pop into Ed Arayan's Department Store. They still called it that, even though old Ed had died some years before, leaving the business to his widow. What a store! We'd get down on our knees in front of the glass counters and ogle the strange and fascinating collection of pocket-knives, compasses, and bizarre musical instruments that the Arayans had assembled. In one display, there was a whole collection of harmoniphones—long instruments that you blew into with piano-style keyboards along the side. It always seemed to us that it would be a cinch to master the instrument—if any of us could have ever afforded one.

Unlike the Five-and-Dime ladies, Mrs. Arayan didn't seem to mind the daily visitation of little boys. When one of us asked to see one of the "genuine pearl-handled" jackknives, she would roll out a small velvet mat and present the article with all the sober dignity of a jewelry salesman showing diamonds to a wealthy client. "Oh, yah," she would say in her heavy German accent, "fine qual-i-tee." As a matter of fact, everything in her whole store was "fine qual-i-tee."

Another business owner who saw a lot of traffic from the sneaker set was George, owner of The Newsstand. It probably had another name—the Placerville News Company or some such thing—but everyone in town just called it The Newsstand. It was one of those old buildings from the Gold Rush days, with the original, creaky wood floors and an ancient ceiling fan, spinning away up above. The floorboards felt wonderfully cool to bare feet that had been dancing across scalding concrete sidewalks. While you cooled your heels at George's place, you could check out the latest comic books and baseball cards—or maybe invest in a jumbo Tootsie Roll.

Placerville in the fifties and early sixties was a slow, sleepy, safe place to live. No one worried about kids out on their own, having the run of the town. There were no malls, no McDonald's, no cell phones or beepers, no gangs or graffiti. Commuters from sprawling Sacramento had not yet begun to absorb the town as a bedroom community. It was still small-town America, right out of a Norman Rockwell painting, and was a wonderful place for a boy to explore and roam with his buddies.

LOVE AT FIRST SIGHT

Nothing too monumental happened in my early years—beyond absorbing the comfortable rhythms of an old-fashioned American small town. My mother and father parted ways when I was very young, and my brother, Pat, and I grew up in a single-parent home. Riding my bike around town on a summer night, or maybe walking home from school on a dusky winter afternoon, I would always find myself drawn to the warm glow of windows in the homes I passed. I always tried to imagine what was going on behind those windows...the laughter, the conversations, the horseplay, the hearty family meals around dining-room tables.

The windows in my own home were often dark, my mother hard at work (often until late in the evening) supporting the family. From those very early days of childhood, I've always been drawn in by the buttery yellow light pouring out of friendly windows and the smoke curling out of a chimney. They've become a hallmark of my paintings.

Maybe that's why I particularly enjoyed being a paperboy from age eleven on. Besides the pocket money it afforded, going from street to street, house to house, yard to yard, was endlessly interesting to me. You could tell a great deal about people from the way they kept their lawns or gardens, by looking into an open garage door, or perhaps by the toys lying out in the front yards. Now and then, you could catch a whiff of dinner cooking: spaghetti at the Wards', Mrs. Rossi's meat loaf and fresh bread—or chocolate chip cookies—at the Reeses'.

But it was a chance encounter on Fairview Drive that would change my life forever.

The Willeys were new in town, and as I sailed down the road to toss a free sample onto their porch, I saw a pretty blond-headed girl about my age sitting on the front step. On that particular day, I decided against firing the folded paper against the front door with my usual pinpoint accuracy. On that day, the paper would be hand-delivered.

The girl's name, I took care to find out, was Nanette.

Nanette: 🌿

*O*ur family had just moved to Placerville. My father had been on an assignment overseas in the Philippines. It was a hot day, and I was sitting out on the front steps with one of my favorite books when I suddenly looked up and saw a gangly teenage boy pulling up in front of our house on his bicycle, delivering papers.

He smiled, introduced himself as Thom Kinkade, politely handed me the folded paper, and took off down the street. It was one of those times that you read about in stories or see in old movies but have difficulty believing.

We fell in love. We truly did. At first sight.

Thom was thirteen and I was twelve. And through the years we've always agreed on one thing: From that moment in front of my house on Fairview Drive, we knew that—somehow, in some inexplicable way—we were going to be together the rest of our lives.

The very next day we met again. It was a funny incident that did not seem at all funny to me at the time.

I had planned to walk down to the high school swimming pool with the girl from next door. Knowing that she was coming by for me at any minute, I donned my brand-new bikini. When the doorbell rang, I thought it would be fun to show off a little. I threw open the door with a grand gesture, opened my arms wide, and shouted, "Ta-daaaa!"

Only it wasn't my friend.

It was Thom, soliciting for the newspaper. He was standing there with a surprised, somewhat dazzled expression on his face. Being the mature twelve-year-old that I was, I screamed and hid behind the door.

I think Thom and I were just enamored with each other in those early days. As time went on, we saw energy and creativity in one another. Thom was immediately drawn to our family. Because we'd traveled a great deal and had lived overseas, we had a number of unique decorations and furnishings around the house—and a wealth of experiences and interesting tales to tell. Compared to life in provincial Placerville, we must have seemed glamorous and exotic.

Coming straight from several years in the Philippines, I didn't dress like any girl he'd ever seen. All of my clothes had been hand-tailored and embroidered by Filipino seamstresses (which is about the only way you could get clothes over there). Thom, romantic even in those early days of preadolescence, was completely enchanted. And I, a new girl in town, enjoyed having such a receptive audience for my stories about where we had lived and the things we had done.

Besides being flattered by Thom's rapt attention, I was impressed with his self-confidence and unique outlook on life. Who ever heard of a paperboy who talked about painters and carried a sketchbook with him on his route? The more we talked, the more amazed I became at how ambitious and goal oriented he seemed to be. At the age of thirteen, he already knew what he wanted to do in life. He knew he wanted to be an artist, and he knew the kind of lifestyle he wanted to live.

As we jumped and bounced together on our family trampoline in the backyard, Thom told me he wanted to travel, have adventures, and do things that were out of the ordinary—

> *He was standing there with a surprised, somewhat dazzled expression on his face.*

or "out of the box," as he would later explain it.

I had goals, too. I wanted to be a nurse, eventually become a wife and mother, and devote myself to caring for a family. So we talked a lot about those goals and dreams. I think that's how we became such good friends: We talked continually about everything. As time went on, we really came to understand each other and communicate on an even deeper level. As we spent hours on the trampoline, on the front porch, and delivering Thom's papers in the neighborhood together, we began to feel like soul mates in our dreams for our futures.

This is all very odd for us to think about now, because we have a twelve-year-old daughter. She is very mature and responsible and loves the Lord with all her heart. But Thom and I can't imagine her having that same vision of a very specific future the way we did. I think God just put that in our hearts at an early age because He knew He had a plan for us together. ✿

FIRST DATE

Nanette: 🦋

*I*t makes me smile to recall that as bold and outgoing as Thomas was as a young teenager, *I* was the one who asked *him* on our first date. Not long after we met, our junior high school had a Sadie Hawkins Day dance, and I invited the paperboy.

I'd understood that Sadie Hawkins Day is the day when girls get to invite boys to a dance. What I hadn't understood is that we were to be "married" at that dance—as the girls dragged their dates in front of a "country preacher" (one of our classmates in tails, top hat, and a phony mustache). Now I was embarrassed. But as we were waiting in line, I was even more aghast when I saw that part of the mock marriage ceremony involved "kissing the bride"—right there in front of everyone.

I'd never kissed a boy in my life, and I found myself thinking, *Oh, my gosh. What is Thom going to think? What am I going to do?* I was as nervous as could be. Then Thom looked over at me with a twinkle in his eye and slipped his arm around my shoulders. In a very cool and debonair voice he leaned toward me and whispered, "Wanna practice?" Without waiting for my answer, he bent his head over and kissed me. Right on the lips, too! So our first kiss was right there in the line. A few minutes later, Thom and I kissed for the second time as the preacher pronounced us "man and wife." And that was the end of the kissing for a good long time! ✿

THE STORY OF MY friendship with Nanette in Placerville is really a dream vision of an innocent childhood romance. This was an era of our lives before sexual awareness. There was never any impropriety in our relationship—we didn't even know what that was. We just became soul mates as we shared our dreams and desires for the future. Though we were unaware of it at the time, we were really laying the foundation for our love story and a lifelong companionship. We developed friendship, trust, communication, and mutual dreams—tools that would one day help us build our lives together into one.

REDISCOVERED LOVE

Nanette and I remained friends through high school, dating only occasionally. It was more like a brother-sister relationship. We knew each other so well and shared so many common childhood memories and experiences.

After graduation, our dreams seemed to lead us in different directions—she to nursing school and me to Cal Berkeley and eventually to art school. Each of us had dated here and there throughout high school and college, but nothing had clicked. We both had some vague ideas about leaving the confines of our small town and "expanding our horizons." In the intervening years, we immersed ourselves in our studies, developed new friendships, and established new routines. Our horizons were certainly wider, but—something felt missing.

My small-town Christian faith was at first challenged and later confirmed by my experiences at the university. Following a period of confusion and searching, I committed my life to Christ in a deeply intimate way. The renewal of faith is perhaps the most vibrant of personal experiences, and I suddenly found my life and my art energized with fresh passion and a strong desire to bring glory to my Creator and Savior.

After leaving Cal, I headed to the Art Center College of Design in Southern California and eventually landed a job in North Hollywood working for the movie industry. I now spent long days doing background paintings for films, keeping my own work alive by sketching and painting on evenings and weekends. It was a busy time, a fulfilling time, and a perfect foundation for my career as the "Painter of Light." I knew that some of my contemporaries from art school hadn't been able to find a job in the arts. Instead of sharpening their skills and building a portfolio, they were selling insurance, working in some gray cubicle in a high-rise office building, or maybe managing a fast-food place along a busy street.

I had much to be thankful for. So why did I find myself so...restless at times? It was as though something kept trying to remind me of another dream, another vision—something long hidden but never quite forgotten.

Placerville? It all seemed so long ago and far away.

Nanette? I hadn't even thought of her for at least a year.

And then one night I had the closest thing to a vision I've ever experienced.

"FOLLOW YOUR HEART"

I woke up one workday morning with the vivid memory of having called Nanette.

I could clearly remember talking to her. The gladness in her voice. The laughter. The long talk about old times. I'd told her about my new job, my passion for Christ, and my vision for a new style of light-filled painting.

Sitting up in bed, I was alarmed to realize that I couldn't remember *when* I had called her, *when* we had talked. Last night? The night before? Why could I remember the conversation—the emotions—so clearly, but not the circumstances of that conversation?

Or—had we even talked at all?

The vividness and compelling nature of the dream forced me to contemplate: Could this be a sign from God? If it was just a dream, I'd never had one so realistic, so gripping. I found myself physically aching to talk to her some more, to find out what was going on in her life, to find out if she still remembered our childhood dreams of being together.

The next day at work, as I painted alongside a good friend in the studio, I told him about my experience. "What should I do?" I asked him. "Should I call her? Get back in touch? I don't even know for sure where she is. I don't even have a phone number."

He put down his brush and looked me.

"Thom, just follow your heart."

I did.

I followed my heart that very moment: I got up from my brushes and paints and went to the telephone. I did have one phone number—one I still knew by heart. Her old home number in Placerville.

> *I found myself physically aching to talk to her some more.*

I dialed it. The phone began ringing.

Surely she was at college, I thought.

Perhaps she was married.

Maybe she was overseas.

She couldn't possibly be at home…in Placerville.

"Hello," a voice said.

Beyond all hope, it was Nanette.

We began talking together—yakking away and laughing as if the years apart had never happened. We might as well have been back on her front porch on Fairview Drive—or jumping on the trampoline. She had left school just a week or so before and returned home after a serious accident that left her with a severely broken leg. She too had gone through a period of deep searching and had recently been spending a lot of time in prayer for her life. In fact, the night of my dream she had been praying that God would bring the right man into her life—never realizing that it might be a one-time paperboy and up-and-coming artist by the name of Kinkade.

> *She had been praying that God would bring the right man into her life.*

Just that morning Nanette had been discouraged over the turns her life had taken. How had things become so messed up? She'd gone off to college with high ideals and expectations. She'd thought, *If I can just get out of this little town for a while, I'll get a chance to meet new people and discover all kinds of new and exciting things.* But now, looking back, her experiences seemed flat—

like stale soda. So many of the people she'd been around talked only about making money or chasing a good time. It all seemed so shallow.

And then there was the accident. The pain. The uncertainty. The long days flat on her back. She'd had to leave her studies, move back home. And what was ahead? Her doctors had even warned her that she might never walk again.

So here came this telephone call from her long-lost childhood sweetheart. Thom was dropping into her life once again, right out of the blue Placerville sky.

"Nanette," I found myself saying, "why don't we go up to Lake Tahoe this weekend? We could go out to dinner. Maybe see a show or go dancing? What do you say? I'll pick you up in my new car."

"Sounds great!" she answered.

She hung up the phone thinking, *How am I going to go dancing with crutches and a full-length leg cast?* And as I hung up I began thinking, *Fine. Now all I have to do is go buy a car.*

I didn't even own a broken-down used car at the time—let alone a new one. All I had was my banged-up Honda motorcycle. That would never fly for an elaborate date with the girl of my dreams—especially when that girl had a broken leg and crutches.

So I went out and bought a car that week in preparation for Saturday night. One I thought Nanette would like. And bright and early Saturday morning, I put that little car through its paces and drove 425 miles to Placerville, picked up Nanette, and then drove another 60 miles up to Lake Tahoe.

Ten hours of nonstop driving, yet I felt as fresh as a meadow flower.

I took her to a swanky restaurant on top of a lakeside hotel. The place had floor-to-ceiling windows and a view of that whole magnificent lake under a golden summer moon. We talked nonstop through dinner; then as the orchestra group began playing romantic tunes, we slow-danced in the middle of the dance floor—Nanette in cast and crutches, but in my arms at last. The whole restaurant loved it, and everyone cleared the floor as we swayed with the music. Patrons began applauding after every dance, and the bandleader dedicated several songs to "the lovely lady on crutches."

We fell in love all over again and wiled away the night driving around the moonlit lake, recalling old friends and bygone times. We ended up at an all-night coffee shop, where we grabbed a bag of bagels, then found our way down to the beach, where we sipped coffee and watched the sun rise over the water.

After wandering the beach for hours, hand in hand, we drove the scenic route back to good old Placerville, where I dropped Nanette off in time for dinner—after a date nearly twenty-four hours long! With a quick hug of farewell, I hit the freeway for Southern California and drove all night, arriving at the movie studio parking lot in time to begin my painting shift. I hadn't slept in who knows how long, but hey, what's coffee for anyway? Even without the caffeine, I was energized in a way I hadn't known for years. All my dreams were falling into place, and God Himself had assembled the pieces. I knew that if Nanette and I could be together—no matter what else happened or didn't happen in my art career—I was in for a life that was eminently worth living.

On our second date, I confessed my love to Nanette and said what we'd both thought in the backs of our minds since we were children: "Nanette, I just think we were meant to be together."

Looking into my eyes, she took a deep breath and said, "Yes, Thom, I agree. I think we're supposed to be together."

"Okay," I said. "Well, now what?"

And with that, we began planning our wedding.

With all my heart, I believe our coming back together was a sovereign act of God. We'd shared a dream together when we were just a couple of kids. But through the years, we'd lost sight of that dream. It had been so real in our hearts at one time, but as life goes on, there's an inevitable erosion that takes place. Dreams are like a fire in your fireplace; you can't leave the house, run a dozen errands, and expect the fire to keep burning merrily on its own. A fire must be tended. It's the same with dreams. If you don't pursue them, garner them up, treasure them, and build upon them through the years, they'll wane and fade. If you don't guard them from the push and pull and pressures of life—the constant exigencies and urgencies and responsibilities—you'll be left with a cold hearth and the ashes of "what might have been."

ROLLER SKATES AND ROSES

Now that Nanette and I had declared our love for one another, I wasn't about to let those dreams languish. Even though we were still separated by many miles, we planned elaborate experiences together.

On one such date, I picked her up in Placerville at seven in the morning, and we drove to San Francisco. We didn't get back until late that night, and those hours were filled to the brim with incredible, serendipitous, almost miraculous experiences together. We roller-skated through the city's rose gardens, chatted with an old sea captain down on the wharf, and dined on fresh cracked-crab for dinner as the sunset painted the Bay with colors I've longed to find on my own palette. We surprised an old friend in Berkeley and ate double-scoop ice cream cones at a famous ice cream parlor. It was experience piled upon experience—a time of building memories so vivid that they would resist the erosion of time.

> *Hours were filled to the brim with incredible, serendipitous, almost miraculous experiences together.*

Back at work after our date, I drew a little comic book, illustrating our escapades in the City by the Bay. I titled it "The Adventures of Thom and Nanette" and mailed it off to her. We still have that little book somewhere, but we haven't really needed it as a reminder. All we have to do is close our eyes and the memories play all over again in Technicolor and Dolby surround sound.

When we got married, those shared experiences formed some of the superglue that bonded us together. Throughout the years of our relationship, we've both placed a high value on experience. On building memories. Given the choice between an experience or a possession, I'll take the experience every time. After all, possessions come and go. Possessions lose their luster and wear out. But an experience lasts for a lifetime, gaining radiance and joy with each retelling.

COUNTRY WEDDING

Nanette:

Even as children, we knew we were going to be together. We had determined that we would live what at that time we called "a country life."

One of the clear advantages of a relaxed, country wedding is that it doesn't cost much. In fact, it *couldn't* cost much because we had no money— and neither did my parents, who might have been expected to help with the funding. But it was by far the best wedding I've ever attended (and not just because I happened to be the bride).

We were married in the little community of Coloma, near the South Fork of the American River. The South Fork made history back in 1848 with the discovery of gold under its waters. Thom designed and illustrated our wedding invitation. On the inside he wrote: "Where gold will be discovered for the *second* time."

The wedding took place in a little white country church house, built in the 1850s, on the grounds of the Marshall Gold Discovery Historic State Park. It was all very relaxed—and so much fun! One of the pastors who mentored Thom as a boy married us, and we had a little barbecue afterward in the picnic area. There was no stiffness, no pretense. Everything was as relaxed as it could be. The men wore black denim trousers and dark suspenders over white, Sunday-go-to-meeting, long-sleeved dress shirts, and the women wore calico country dresses. For the flowers, my mother gathered wildflowers and arranged them in mason jars. We hired a local bluegrass band to play during the reception and served sparkling cider out in the warm California sunshine.

> *My mother gathered wildflowers and arranged them in mason jars.*

After the wedding, we got into our little pickup and headed for a campground near the seaside village of Mendocino. We slept on a mattress in the camper shell at the rear of our truck, happily saving our money for the last two nights of luxury at a little bed-and-breakfast on the coast.

If we'd had all the money in the world, we couldn't have been more jubilant than we were that week. We had waited for each other—waited for this moment—since we were kids on the rural lanes of Placerville. And now, in the kindness of God, we walked the long beaches of Mendocino as husband and wife.

Life was beginning all over again, and it was good.

It still is.

MOONLIT BIKE RIDES

Nanette:

After our honeymoon we returned to Thom's tiny apartment in a rundown section of Los Angeles that was favored by artists. Living in an urban slum would probably have been viewed as a low point for most couples. But the glow of love made everything alive and new. Besides, we didn't have time to notice our surroundings—we were having too much fun.

I was starting my first job as an RN at a big hospital, so of course I was assigned to the night shift. In order for us to operate on the same schedule, Thom decided to become a "night painter." So we worked all night and slept through the day. In our free time together, we'd shop at all-night groceries, visit libraries and free museums, and bike-ride all over our neighborhood.

AS I LOOK BACK ON some of those days, I wonder if we were just a little crazy.

Bike-riding through L.A. ghettos by moonlight?

But we enjoyed ourselves immensely. Maybe it was like being kids again, delivering papers in Placerville. As we pedaled through the poor neighborhoods and graffiti-covered alleyways, we could catch glimpses into people's lives. It was fascinating—an intricate tapestry of human experience and intertwined lives.

We would ride for hours, exploring new streets and new neighborhoods every night. In the afternoon, after working an all-night shift, we made a ritual of going out to eat at some little café or diner. For over a year and a half, the Kinkades would go to bed at seven in the morning and eat dinner for breakfast.

Nanette: ❧

When I wasn't on duty at the hospital, I would help Thom any way I could: preparing his painting panels, stretching canvases, putting together presentation portfolios, and all the other little tasks that would allow him to spend more time painting.

A big part of our adventures in those days was putting together our weekend one-man art shows and hitting the road in our little truck and camper. One weekend it might be Tucson, the next San Francisco or La Jolla. We slept in our camper and had to do everything on a very tight budget, but that's the way both of us had grown up, so it didn't bother us at all.

More and more people began to recognize and appreciate the art of Thomas Kinkade, and it was a thrill to share all those experiences together—the highs and lows, the days when we found ourselves with a few extra dollars and the days when we wondered how we'd make it through the month.

There was always laughter.

There was always adventure.

And there was always each other.

Our long friendship had flowered into romantic love, and twenty years later the fragrance remains.

It's still great fun to be in love. ❦

We long for
something lasting
in a world that
constantly moves,
shifts, and changes.

CHAPTER TWO

An Enduring Love

W hat if you had the power to suddenly freeze time and capture a single moment of life? What if you could turn it in your hands like a multi-faceted jewel? What if you could hold it up to the light, peer into its depths, and ponder its mysteries?

Most of us, at one time or another, have longed for such an ability.

We're creatures of time, but as Solomon wrote, God has set eternity in our hearts. We ache for something lasting in a world that constantly moves, shifts, and changes. We're residents of a madly whirling sphere hurtling through the void at unimagined speed. Time rushes us along in a dark current of mystery.

That's why we wish we could stop it all sometimes—even if just for a few ticks of the cosmic clock. Every now and then, we experience a moment we just ache to hang onto for a while, holding its fragrance, drinking in its joy, savoring its tang on our tongues.

You step outside your door as the last drops of a spring shower wash across the landscape. You breathe deeply of cool, fresh air just as a shaft of sunlight pierces the clouds and illumines the treetops half a mile away.

You walk along a lakeshore at twilight, looking up at the instant the sun slips behind the mountains, outlining the peaks—for a breathless moment—in molten gold.

You stand with your fly rod in the crystal current of a trout stream, the air redolent of sun-warmed pine. You've just made the perfect cast, your fly dancing in rippled diamonds.

You're having a picnic in a meadow, on a faded quilt, sipping good coffee from a red thermos cup. Your little daughter reclines in an infant seat beside you, sucking apple juice from a baby bottle. A tiny breeze riffles her wispy hair. She pulls the nipple from her mouth, looks right into your eyes, and dazzles you with a smile of boundless joy.

The moment. The wild, sweet, exultant moment. It touches you, teases you, then passes you by, forever out of reach. You may encounter other similar moments in your life, but never another instant just like *that*. That particular alignment of life belongs to the past. It has flowed on downstream and will never return.

Painting is all about capturing and holding such moments.

As an artist, I strive to freeze time, to stop life in its tracks. Through my paintings, God has enabled me to grasp the fleeting and make it endure. It's as though I can take a single tick of the clock and make it timeless. I try to grab that elusive perfect moment and hold onto it for years, passing it on to others who can in turn hold it, treasure it, project themselves into its beauty, and experience the wonder all over again. Where a photographer may wait for years to capture such a moment, to create such depth in a single instant, the artist gives it birth at his leisure.

THE CHANGING...AND THE CHANGELESS

I am fascinated with the interplay between the changing and the changeless in my artwork. Every Thomas Kinkade painting you'll ever see represents a moment in time—a slice of life, the split second of a perfect moment—distilled onto a rectangle of canvas.

Within that arrested moment you will see both the enduring and the temporal...that which alters shape in the twinkling of an eye and that which stands for ten thousand years.

> *The person you married is constantly changing. And by the way... so are you.*

Life, of course, is a succession of such moments; it's a strung-together cluster of the constantly changing dynamic we call experience. Just as a great river is constantly in motion, so change is constant in our lives. In each of my paintings you will see that which is in the very process of changing, as well as those things that do not change. Perhaps it will be a street scene in Paris, seventy-five years ago, just before dusk. People drive their cars, stroll along the sidewalks, or stop for a moment at a shop window, illumined by its glow.

If you could advance that frame a moment or two, the cars will have moved on. The people will have walked by. The particular pattern of sunlight in the clouds or in the reflection of the rain-washed streets will have faded and changed.

In a landscape, the light will change; the shadows will move; the clouds will rearrange; a curling wisp of mist will disappear almost as soon as it forms. Yet the mountains remain. The rivers flow on for centuries. The granite cliffs endure through countless seasons.

I love to portray such moments in my paintings. To capture a changing world and render it changeless.

But I can't do that in my life.

I can't do that in my marriage.

Unlike the motionless world of a painting, marriage—and life itself—is constantly changing. It must be so, for (have you noticed?) the person you married is constantly changing.

And by the way...so are you.

MYSTERIES AND CERTAINTIES

I read somewhere that every cell in your body renews itself over a process of seven years—from the cells of your big toe to the cells deep within your brain. That physical person you see in the mirror isn't the same one that looked back at you just seven years ago.

Change is part of the mystery of life. There are factors in your marriage that are a mystery at the time you take your vows.

You may marry someone in perfect health, only for him or her to develop severe physical, mental, or emotional problems just a few years later. You may stand at the altar with an easygoing soul, someone with a ready laugh and smile. Yet the stresses of life (and who knows what they will be?) can change that. Scripture reminds us that "by sorrow of heart the spirit is broken" (Proverbs 15:13, RSV). And who can say when the spirit is mended?

People change, don't they? Sometimes for the worse, but sometimes for the better, too. You may marry someone you're very sure never wanted any children, only to find out that he or she is the best dad or mom you've ever encountered.

That was certainly true in my case. Nanette knew I was a bit indifferent about starting a family. I didn't discover how much I would thoroughly enjoy little ones (four daughters, at that!) until they waltzed into my heart and took over. It's not that I had anything against children. I thought they were fine at a safe distance—like some exotic animal at the zoo. I just didn't want to climb in the same cage with them.

But now I can't imagine life without my girls. Each one of them is an inexpressible delight to me. Being "Dad" is one of the best things about being alive. I've changed and my heart has expanded fourfold—who could have predicted it?

That's just it. Nobody can predict what will happen in a marriage. The simple fact of aging creates change. Your needs, your experiences, and your perspectives will be different in every successive season of life. Your fortunes may change dramatically. You may begin marriage with what you thought was a secure nest egg, only to find that a spate of business setbacks or medical bills has left you with nothing. On the other hand, you may find yourself blessed with resources beyond your most outrageous dreams. We've had many friends whose major goal in life was to raise a big family. Yet what they had planned on so intently wasn't meant to be. But who can

> *My heart has expanded fourfold— who could have predicted it?*

say what adventures and challenges await a family without children—or with one child instead of the desired four or five? Life can certainly be as sweet for a small family as for a large one.

Think of the families who lives were disrupted or displaced by World War II, or the Great Depression—events beyond their control. You and I can't know those things going into a marriage. You don't know where you'll be a month from now, let alone in ten years. What did the apostle say?

> *You do not even know what will happen tomorrow. What is your life? You are a mist that appears for a little while and then vanishes.*
>
> JAMES 4:14

There are so many things Nanette and I don't know—and cannot know. Thank the Lord, we're all in good health as I write these words. Our business has prospered beyond our fondest hopes. We're all fulfilled, busy, and happy.

This moment, this slice of life, delights me beyond telling. But we can't seal it up in amber. We can't freeze it in time like a painting on a canvas. Just as we've begun to take pleasure in one "era" in the Kinkade family, we've moved on to another. And another and another, each with its own blessings and trials. Life sweeps on by, and there are no guarantees.

Even so, there are those things that do not change...fixed points in a turning world.

WHAT DOESN'T CHANGE

What stays the same in a marriage?

God stays the same.

The One who created you and gave you to each other never changes. The Bible tells us that "every good and perfect gift is from above, coming down from the Father of the heavenly lights, who does not change like shifting shadows" (James 1:17). The book of Hebrews declares that "Jesus Christ is the same yesterday and today and forever" (Hebrews 13:8).

No matter what happens in your life, no matter what happens in the life of your spouse or your children, no matter what happens across this whole wide world, God remains eternally the same. His promises are unshakable. The One who stood ready to help you on the day of your wedding is still available, still loves you, and still has power to calm any storm.

What else stays the same?

Your vows stay the same.

That's why the traditional wedding vows are worded the way they are. "*To love and to cherish...forsaking all others...in sickness and in health...for richer, for poorer...so long as you both shall live.*"

Wedding vows speak of unchanging realities in a world that reinvents itself with every passing hour. The promises you made to each other, in time and space, before the solemn scrutiny of the eternal God and the witness of family and friends, remain. The vows precede the multitude of mysteries in a marriage and go with you through those mysteries.

> *Wedding vows speak of unchanging realities in a world that reinvents itself with every passing hour.*

Many things have changed in the lives of Thom and Nanette Kinkade since we exchanged vows in that little church in Coloma, California, twenty years ago. We had very little then but each other. We had our love, we had our dreams, and we had a relationship with the living God through Jesus Christ.

Beyond those inexpressible riches, we didn't possess very much of this world's stuff. A tiny apartment. A depleted bank account. A little pickup truck with a leaky camper shell on back. A couple of bikes. A room crammed with painting supplies.

Yet on that golden day in California's Gold Rush country, Nanette Willey and I vowed to be faithful to each other…*come what may*. We pledged to stand by each other, to love and cherish each other…*no matter what*.

Other things may change, but that does not change, will not change. Events beyond our reckoning may turn our world upside down, but our promises before heaven remain in full effect. God knows that, Nanette knows that, I know that, and our daughters know that. Those vows are the enduring mountains, the granite cliffs in the painting of our lives.

ANCHORS OF CONSTANCY

One of the constants in our marriage is the simple fact that Nanette and I just love to be together. And we *cultivate* that togetherness.

It's true. We'd rather be with each other than with anyone else in all the world. We've enjoyed being together since we were kids. I have a mental image of us from when we were twelve and thirteen. We had walked to downtown Placerville to look at stuff in the stores—and maybe buy a bag of that good ten-cent popcorn at the Ben Franklin Five-and-Dime. As we started home, it began to rain. One of us got the bright idea of asking for a large plastic garbage bag at the little grocery store. With a pair of borrowed scissors, we cut out a hole for our two heads in the top, and a hole on each side for one of our arms—my left, her right. Then we slipped the bag over us and—voilá!—the perfect temporary raincoat.

What a sight we must have been—a four-legged, two-headed creature lurching along the sidewalks of Placerville in the rain, munching soggy popcorn...and laughing all the way home.

That desire to be together has never changed. But we haven't taken it for granted. Instead, we've made a point to enhance it and pursue it as a constant in our marriage. We seek each other out because we love being together.

Together! Isn't that why we married? Isn't that why we left the "freedom" of single life behind? We wanted proximity. We wanted to be close. We felt elated to be near one another.

It's been that way since the beginning of our romance. Every moment I could spend with Nanette was the most precious moment I could imagine. When we were dating, I would drive twelve hours from Southern California to Chico just to spend two hours with her—and then drive twelve hours home. We would go out on a date in Chico, lingering till the last possible moment. And then I'd kiss her good night and drive all night to get back to my studio, just in time to go to work.

Now someone might say, "Crazy kids. People do the dumbest things when they're young and in love." Yes, but now I'm middle-aged and in love, and time with this woman is just as precious to me as it was years ago.

> *Cultivate the delight of simply being together and make it a constant in your marriage*

Sometimes, because we now have four children, it takes a little more planning than it did in the old days. But because of our commitment to cultivate togetherness, we take the time to make arrangements and get away together on a regular basis—maybe for a weekend, maybe for dinner, maybe just for a walk in the park. It doesn't really matter where it is, as long as we're together.

We don't have a TV in our home to rob us of time with each other in the evenings. We don't have a lot of outside commitments or social obligations that pull us apart night after night. We've deliberately avoided hobbies and pastimes that might take us in different directions.

It's not that I couldn't go golfing with the guys if I wanted to, or that Nanette couldn't go to aerobics or go shopping with a group of women friends. That's not the point. The point is that we look for ways to be together and to develop mutual interests. If I want to golf, I prefer to do so with my wife; if Nanette enrolls in an aerobics class, I'm her first choice as a workout partner. At the same time, we're on guard against those activities that might rob us of time with one another or draw us apart.

You don't have to let that desire for togetherness fade. You don't have to let the sparkle and enchantment grow flat. You can cultivate the delight of simply being together and make it a constant in your marriage...one of those things that does not change in a changing world.

KEEPERS OF THE FLAME

It is the very fact of change in a marriage that leads so many men and women to abandon the relationship at some point and go their separate ways. Someone will say, "Well, he's changed." Or, "She's changed." Or maybe, "I've changed, and I just don't feel the same way about my spouse that I used to. So I guess it's time to leave. I guess it's time to re-create those feelings I used to have with someone new."

I'd like to compare this sort of logic with something I really know about. Depending on the changeable emotions in a marriage is like an artist who might say, "I just don't *feel* any inspiration today. I don't *feel* anything at all. I guess I won't paint today. I'll wait until the mood comes upon me, and then I'll pick up my brush."

That's an artist who will never accomplish anything. You could wait a lifetime for "inspiration" to show up on your doorstep or drop out of the clouds.

I meet people all the time who have this crazy impression about art. They apparently think an artist is one who wanders around seeking inspiration. And then when that divine moment arrives, when the muses suddenly speak, you have to run to the studio and create a piece of art before those mystic vibrations fade away. You have to seize the moment.

It's true that inspiration does come to me at unexpected times and in unexpected ways. I can't predict it. I can't schedule it. I can't put it in my Day-Timer for eight o'clock, Tuesday morning. For that reason, I certainly can't base my livelihood on something that might be here today and gone tomorrow. You might read romantic stories about "starving artists," but I've been there, and it's no fun. Now I have a wife and four daughters to support, so there's no way I'm going to sit out in the garden with my eyes closed waiting for some will-o'-the-wisp revelation to descend.

I go to work every morning, just like everyone else.

I get to the studio by seven or eight, sit down at my easel, and work all day long at my painting. (My apologies if this shatters some romantic image you might have developed.) Inspiration, as it comes on any given day, will come because I have sat myself down in front of a canvas and picked up a brush. *It will come because I have put myself in position to receive it.* I have disciplined myself to simply be there, rain or shine, good day or bad day, cheerful or crabby, pressured or peaceful, feeling good or feeling sick. I'm on task every day, with the exception of Sunday, which I take off for worship and for time with my family.

And believe it or not, when I show up, inspiration comes.

In fact, sometimes a vision burns in my heart like white fire, and I can hardly paint fast enough to get it on canvas.

> *And where do those feelings come from? Do they fall out of the sky?*

Because of my discipline, I've put myself in position to be an "inspired artist." And because Nanette and I have practiced certain disciplines in our marriage, we have put ourselves in a position to enjoy a romantic love that's blossomed over twenty years.

Practice the act, and the inspiration comes.

Practice the act, and romance returns.

Someone says, "Well, it's different at our house. I don't feel romantic toward my wife anymore."

And I will reply, "That's interesting. Tell me, when was the last time you planned an extravagant evening, for just the two of you?"

"You don't understand. That's my problem. I don't feel like doing that. The sparkle is gone. I don't feel that magnetic attraction anymore."

And where do those feelings come from? Do they fall out of the sky? Do they vibrate your heart like frequencies on some elusive radio band? What if you started *doing* things that might invite romance back into your relationship? Maybe something like this… You book reservations for you and your wife at the best restaurant with the nicest view of the city. You call ahead to a florist and have flowers waiting there when you arrive. You buy a sparkly copy-jewelry bracelet for twenty-five dollars and drop it into the bouquet, along with a card. You open the door for her, pull out her chair for her. You sit down at that table and order your favorite meal. You've thought through some things to talk about as you dine. You live some of your most memorable moments all over again. You laugh over some of your craziest dating memories. You hold her hand as you take a walk after dinner.

So what am I saying here? That you have to spend a pile of money and go in debt for a single date? No, I'm simply making the point that you need to put yourself in a position for the "inspiration" to come. Make provision for it. Create space for it. Anticipate it. Pray for it. And yes, sacrifice a little to achieve it. Unfailingly, if you do all these things—even if you had thought it was a lost cause with your spouse—you will begin to feel something. And so will she.

Picture this dinner date with your husband or wife as your first date, and here is this person you have dreamed of going out with. Before you know it, it starts being fun again, and you begin to recover some of that childlike joy.

FANTASIES AND REALITIES

Sometimes it amazes me how predictable the pattern is in failed marriages. People get a divorce, link up with someone new, and suddenly they're doing all of this fun, romantic stuff—moonlight walks and bicycle rides and exotic getaways. They could have done all of those things with the spouse they just left, but they didn't. As a result, they endure the trauma and humiliation of a wrenching divorce, shattering change in their lives, great financial loss, and bitter, deeply wounded children...all for the sake of "new romantic experiences."

Through my business contacts, I've become acquainted with a famous celebrity. Everyone knows his name. The last time I saw him he had some dewy-eyed young model hanging on his arm. He'd left his second wife for this new fling. And not so long before that, he left his first wife for a new romance with the second lady. The other night I was sitting in my living room looking through a magazine, and I came across a picture of this man's first wife.

I said, "What a lovely woman! What in the world was he thinking? Here is this beautiful wife, and he leaves her to run after a younger woman. He stays with her for a few years and then drops her for a still younger girl. And how long do you think *that* relationship will last? Now he's doing all of these wild romantic things with his new girlfriend—cruises, sailing trips, ski weekends at Aspen. What would have happened if he'd stayed with Wife Number One and done all those things with *her* instead? Think of the grief he might have saved. Think of all the confusion, loss, disorientation, and bitterness he might have avoided."

> *If you're going to fantasize and daydream, fantasize and daydream about each other.*

Let me bring it back to art for a moment. I've known painters who have told me that when they move to the mountains, their work will really flourish.

Or perhaps it could be by the seashore. Or the desert. These people spend their lives chasing after some fleeting, ephemeral, emotional "inspiration" to capture on canvas. They spend all their money racing from location to location, chasing it hither and yon and at the end of their days discover a wasted life and a lot of empty canvas.

And by the same token, you could chase the butterfly of romance all over the world, all through your years, from one sexual escapade to another, from one partner to another, and end up at the end of your life as a lonely old person, looking back across the wasteland of empty years.

People fantasize about some racier, more exciting life just over the horizon to be shared with the exciting "someone else." But how much effort have we put into pursuing those same things in our own community and with the person we've come to know best? After all, we certainly used to know how to win the affections of the man or woman that we married. Why do we so often stop doing those things that attracted our spouse and won his or her heart?

The resurrected Lord Jesus said to the believers in Ephesus, "I hold this against you: You have forsaken your first love. Remember the height from which you have fallen! Repent and do the things you did at first" (Revelation 2:4–5).

Jesus was talking about our love for Him and our walk with Him, but the same principle applies to our marriage. We need to hold on to our "first love" with all our hearts in this crazy, changing world. We need to remember what it was like in those early days when we were so head over heels in love with each other. And we need to go back and do those things that we did at the beginning to win and hold each other's love.

If you're going to fantasize and daydream, fantasize and daydream about each other. The fact is, we can make the choice to enjoy the sweetness and fun and laughter with the husband or wife of our youth—with the spouse God gave us. These are the romantic experiences—both carefully planned and spontaneous—that keep a marriage alive, whether you happen to have those "feelings" at the moment or not. You begin to experience romance precisely because you *practice* romance. You practice it deliciously and delightedly with your spouse, inviting fresh inspiration through patient discipline, just as the simple act of picking up the brush does for me as an artist.

TENDER HABITS

The painting process itself generates inspiration and, if you stay at it, begins to create a habit of inspiration. Inspiration grows out of the daily routine of being in the place of inspiration, working as hard as I can. In the same way, feelings of love and romance happen in marriage as we practice the love and kindness and tenderness and creativity that we have developed as habits through the years.

One of the reasons Nanette and I have an exceedingly happy marriage is because we have both practiced these habits day after day, rain or shine, in good times and hard times. My wife wakes up with disheveled hair and no makeup and comes stumbling down the hall in search of the coffeepot, and I say, "Wow, you look gorgeous. What are you doing tonight?"

Nanette walks into my studio when it looks like a volcano has exploded around me and I have stuff strewn all around and spots of paint on my face, and she gives me her sweetest smile. Stepping over the mess, she looks me in the eyes and says, "Did I tell you today how much I love you?"

The fact is, the more you practice these things, the more your wife or husband will become the apple of your eye. Guys, it doesn't really matter if someone else thinks she's beautiful; she can be beautiful in *your* eyes. And the more she sees herself reflected that way in your eyes, the more beautiful she will become.

There was a woman in our Sunday school class who had carried several babies over just a few years. As a result, she became quite overweight—and more than a little distraught by her changed physical appearance. She told our class she'd gone in for counseling because her husband kept telling her how beautiful she was and how much he loved her just the way she was! How could she lose weight, she asked the counselor, when her husband kept telling her he didn't care if she ever lost weight?

Most wives could only dream of having a husband who genuinely thought she was beautiful no matter what her particular age, body shape, or size.

Conversely, I had a friend who was constantly critical of his wife. She worked on her hair all the time, dressed to the hilt, and wore heavy makeup, always trying to find a way to please her nonattentive husband. Underneath all of that, however, she was a genuinely beautiful woman. Some guys in the church and I invited this fellow to a men's retreat. During those hours together, we talked to him about marriage and a wife's emotional needs. Our friend, however, finally admitted he had already planned to throw it all over. He'd made arrangements to leave his wife for a young woman at his office.

His wife was so insecure and uptight, he complained. She wore all that makeup all day—and even put it on before she went to bed. How could he live with such a self-doubting, anxious person?

> *You begin to experience romance precisely because you practice romance.*

Life wasn't any fun with her. He just couldn't seem to make the connection that *he* had created those very fears and anxieties in her heart by his constant criticism and unhappiness with her. If he would begin to compliment her, show tenderness to her, love her, and romance her, he would find a new woman in his home—and it wouldn't be that young woman from the office.

In the process of creating art, I have made the acquaintance of hundreds of artists from across our nation and around the world. Among these, there are a number of men and women whom I call "natural artists." These folks seem to find inspiration wherever they go and can sit down at a moment's notice and begin creating amazing works of art. I've been with artists who could stop the car at a random stoplight, set up their easels, and find something to paint, something inspiring.

Yet there are others who struggle, complain, claim they've got a creative block, and never find inspiration. I remember being with a group of artists in the Sierra Mountains near Yosemite, when several of our group became discouraged because there was "nothing to paint." There we were, on a bluff overlooking the spectacular Yosemite Valley on a bright, sunny day—one of the most majestic settings in all of God's creation—and several of those artists were wandering around, feeling "uninspired" and not knowing what to do.

Inspiration comes to an artist who disciplines himself to practice his craft and remains faithful to his task no matter what. And romantic love—with all the attendant feelings, longings, and desires—comes to those who give themselves to pursuing it through all the days of their marriage..."till death do us part."

TURNING ON THE LIGHTS

Whenever I begin a painting, the first thing I do is lay the foundation. I block in those solid, changeless things first...the mountains, the horizon, the stone bridge across the stream. After all the more solid things are in place, I dip my brush in the golden paint and begin "turning on the lights," adding all the light and sparkle and glow that have become a trademark of my style.

But you can't turn on the lights until you've laid the foundation. In marriage, those foundations are your vows, your daily walk with a loving, unchanging God, your daily kindness and tenderness to one another, and your resolve to give yourselves to your marriage every day with all of your heart.

The shifting, dancing light of joy can reveal itself only on the solid, rocklike foundation of commitment.

*I want to set
hearts yearning for
innocent pleasures
and simpler times.*

CHAPTER THREE

An Exploring Love

O ne of the most gratifying things people ever say about my paintings is that they would like to somehow "step into" a scene I've created and become a part of that little world.

For me as an artist it doesn't get much better than that. It tells me I've created something transcendent. Something that has reached up through the canvas and pigments and called to an individual human soul. Awesome thought!

They've seen a little path winding through a rustic gate into a sun-dappled meadow…and want to follow that trail.

They've seen a rustic road curve through an autumn forest on a mellow afternoon…and hunger to know what lies around the bend.

They've seen a winding stream in the soft, pearly light of morning…and long to sit alongside it on a sun-warmed rock, listen to its voice, and watch the clouds reflected in the water.

They've seen a friendly light glowing though the panes of a mountain cabin at twilight…and wonder what life is like on the other side of that window.

That's been the deep desire of my life since I first picked up a brush. I love to create worlds of beauty where light dances and peace reigns. I want to set hearts yearning for innocent pleasures and simpler times.

Strange as it may sound, I had my own experience of being drawn into a painting not long ago as I was completing a work called "It Doesn't Get Much Better." It's a picture of a man with a fly rod standing atop a log in the current of a trout stream, the morning sun filtering through the summer leaves and glinting off the water. There is no pathway in that scene, but beyond the brook you can just make out a misty meadow. Out past the meadow it's easy to imagine some distant plains…and beyond the plains, the foothills and snowcaps.

Somehow that scene kept drawing me in, even as I added the finishing touches. I kept finding myself pulled into its distances, tugged away from my studio toward that far horizon. What would it be like to set down the fishing pole and just walk into that golden mist shimmering in the distance? What would I find there? What sights, sounds, smells, and sensations might await me? Obviously, since it's a landscape right out of my imagination, no one has ever walked there before. What would it be like to enter your own creation?

> *God gives us one day at a time to discover and experience His good plan for our lives.*

I finally finished that painting. I put down my brush, sent the piece on its way, and began sketching out something new. But in another sense, a true piece of art is never finished. There's always more to be discovered, more to be pondered. If you are drawn to a painting, of course, you have an immediate emotional reaction to it. But as you live with that picture over the course of time, you see things you've never seen before. In a process of unfolding revelation, you begin to interact with the scene before you in a deeper way.

As I've lived over the years with reproductions of some truly great pieces of art—masterworks by artists of the past—I've found myself coming to a point where the painting asks more questions than it answers. The scene portrayed before me, clear and pleasing as it might be, makes me want to look beyond the borders of the picture. What's over that next rise in the distance? What scene awaits just outside that doorway? What lies beyond that bend in the river?

The fascinating element of any pathway is the sense of the undiscovered. And the more you begin to live within a painting in your imagination, the more you find yourself responding to hidden elements, as well as to those plainly revealed. You find yourself as intrigued by what *isn't* shown as you are by the scene itself.

A painting, then, becomes a voyage of discovery, an unfolding story. Each road or pathway in that painting reminds us that we too are travelers on a journey into mystery. God gives us one day at a time to discover and experience His good plan for our lives.

Marriage, too, is a pathway and a mystery.

On that day when you commit your lives to one another, you might imagine that you see quite a bit of what life will be like. Your eyes and your heart are full—even brimming over. But the more time that goes by, the more you realize you've barely started down a road of countless bends, turns, dips, steep ascents, and dazzling vistas.

Marriage is a daily excursion with another person into the unknown. We cannot see beyond the frame of one moment at a time. Yet it is those hidden elements, those mysterious curves in the highway, that draw us along with a sense of anticipation and adventure. The truth is, you can allow that excursion to become flat and predictable, or you can glory in the quest and become explorers with shining eyes who delight in each day's trek.

ADVENTURES SINCE WE WERE KIDS

Nanette: ❧

What is it that makes an adventure? Does it have to be skiing across Antarctica, shooting wild rapids, or scaling some sheer, thousand-foot cliff? It's really a matter of perspective, isn't it? Adventure and delight, after all, are where you find them. For me, at age twelve in the little town of Placerville, riding alongside Thom Kinkade on his paper route rated as a first-class adventure. What fun we had!

Our house on Fairview Drive was one of his first stops, so he'd wheel into our driveway on his Stingray bike, give a little whistle, and I'd be ready to jump on my bike and go with him.

I'll never forget the day when he decided on a whim that we should do the route on his mini-motorbike. He had me sit on the back behind him—although my designated perch seemed a little narrow and precarious. (It's a good thing we were a couple of skinny kids!)

Placerville nestles in the foothills of the Sierras, so a number of residential streets are hilly—with some very steep slopes you wouldn't want to try on a skateboard. As it happens, one of the steepest streets in town was on Thom's route. We started up that hill with Thom's little motorbike revved up as high it could go.

About halfway up, the motorbike *broke in half.*

Just that quickly, we both suddenly found ourselves on unicycles—and then on the pavement—with undelivered copies of the *Sacramento Bee* scattered all about us. It took us a moment to realize that we were both unhurt, and then we both started laughing hysterically. I thought Thom might be upset about his beloved motorbike, but he just shrugged it off with a grin. We'd had an experience and created an unforgettable memory. For Thom, that made it all worthwhile. 🐝

EXPLORATION, DISCOVERY, and serendipity depend more on your attitude and mind-set than on your particular circumstances. You will make discoveries and experience adventures precisely because you are willing to open your eyes and your heart to the *possibility* of discovery and adventure.

Nanette and I learned at an early age that you don't need a lot of money to weave lasting memories. We learned that money—as nice as it may be—isn't necessary to having fun and thoroughly enjoying life.

We had some of our grandest times together

when we were virtually penniless, and we have just as much fun (but not any *more* fun) now that we have four children and God's provision of extra money in the bank.

I have been blessed beyond measure to be married to a woman who delights in simple pleasures and discoveries. Our adventures as a couple have given us priceless opportunities to get to know each other better—to define who we really are as a couple.

Marriage for us isn't a challenge or a struggle or some kind of grim endurance test; it's an everyday adventure. We wake up each day with wide-eyed excitement. Ever since we took off on our camping honeymoon twenty years ago, we've been like Lewis and Clark, setting out across a continent of mystery, discovery, and promise.

Nanette:

When we lived in Los Angeles as newlyweds, we'd hop on our bikes on our days off and set out to explore new neighborhoods, to bike where no Kinkade had gone before.

One day it might be a cruise around the town of Eagle Rock; the next day we'd pedal over to the Huntington Museum in Pasadena—or wherever our whims led us. One late afternoon we found ourselves in the community of Alhambra and turned onto a street called Champion Place. We stopped our bikes and looked at each other. Why did that street name sound so familiar?

Suddenly Thom's eyes lit up. We'd been reading a book about Frank Tenney Johnson, one of our all-time favorite Western artists, who died back in 1939. In the book, he'd mentioned living on Champion Place in Alhambra. Had we actually stumbled onto that very street, just randomly pedaling around neighborhoods? Could we possibly locate his house?

In fact, we did just that. The home pictured in the book was still there—a large, rambling craftsman-style house, at that time a bit overgrown with vines and unpruned trees. At first glance, it reminded me of a dilapidated haunted house. The neighborhood on Champion Place had obviously seen better days. We could only imagine what it must have looked like in its posh glory days of the twenties and thirties.

Johnson, we had read, hosted elaborate dinners and costume parties for his celebrity friends, including artists like Norman Rockwell and actors such as Lionel Barrymore.

We parked our bikes in the long driveway, walked up the steps, and rang the bell. What did we have to lose? At worst, they'd simply tell us to go away—or that they'd never heard of Frank Tenney Johnson.

It turned out, however, that the house was now being rented by a distant relative of the great painter, who seemed more than willing to show us around. Thom and I held hands and walked slowly into the room that had been Frank Tenney Johnson's studio. It was huge with towering walls, dark wood floors, and a mammoth stone fireplace. In that very place, Johnson had

> *When you have joint ownership of a huge treasury of memories, it isn't something you will easily throw away or leave behind.*

created immortal scenes of hard-riding cowboys, blazing gun battles, vast desert ranges, and clear starlit nights by smoldering campfires.

"Just ignore the mess," cautioned our host. As we gazed around we were both startled to see a disassembled motorcycle lying in various parts on the antique Indian rug on the floor. The distant relative had little reverence for the studio of his famous ancestor.

It was a moment we'll never forget. One of those rare rewards, I suppose, for those who are willing to explore life together...and keep their eyes open.

From those earliest days of our marriage, Thom has always managed to squeeze little adventures into our lives—as simple, perhaps, as eating our lunch outside on the lawn, or getting everybody on their bikes after dinner to ride down to the frozen-yogurt shop. He loves that sort of thing, and I've always felt that the winding roads and trails in his work symbolize what he calls his "hobo spirit."

Building memories is part of keeping a marriage alive and growing. The more memories and

experiences you share, the more value your relationship accrues. When you have joint ownership
of a huge treasury of memories, it isn't something
you will easily throw away or leave behind. ❦

WHERE ARE THE MEMORIES?

I've had the great delight of building memories with
Nanette for most of my life. Through it all, we've
learned something important: Memorable experiences
don't happen on their own. They don't come to people
who never venture out, never pry themselves away
from the plastic world of the television set or the com-
forts of their immediate surroundings. You don't see
that double rainbow together unless you happen to be
walking side by side in the rain. You don't stumble
across the forgotten studio of a great artist on an
obscure back street unless you're out roaming the
neighborhoods together on your bikes. You have to
have some element of catalyst. A willingness to break
out of the rut and do something different—maybe a
little crazy. You have to have a basic commitment to
the proposition that marriage is an adventure and that
your lives will be enriched by collecting unique expe-

riences through the years. I've always believed that some of life's most profound lessons, its most over-powering joys, happen when you've put yourself on the path of serendipity.

Sometimes Nanette and I will see an elderly couple sitting in a restaurant together, consuming a meal, and *never saying a word.* They eat, sip their coffee, tap their fingers on the table, look out the window, stare off into space, or bury their noses in a newspaper. It's as though they have nothing whatsoever to talk about. Somehow over the course of time their mutual interests have dwindled from a mingled stream into a shallow puddle—and then dried up altogether. Now, in the final years of their journey, they have nothing left to say, apart from a few mumbled monosyllables.

How tragic! Where are the memories? Where are the wild, crazy, funny, heart-touching moments that ought to arise out of a couple's long trek together through the winding back roads of life?

With God's help, Nanette and I will never allow ourselves to end up in such a situation. We're committed to building memories and gathering experiences—year by year, decade by decade. Someday those memories will keep us reminiscing by winter firesides and on summer evening strolls—even with the help of walking sticks, should God give us length of journey.

The life experience of so many couples I meet has unfortunately become a dull litany of routines. The fun and laughter seems to have gone out of their marriages years ago. But it doesn't have to be that way. Nanette and I have a relationship no different from anyone else's—but we have learned a few secrets of having a dynamic life together.

> *No matter how many pressures or disappointments come into a person's life, you can't let them snuff out the joy.*

For example, though Nanette and I work very, very hard at our tasks of painting, parenting, and household management, we've always got something to anticipate up ahead—some plan to get away or explore or try something new. Those dreams keep us going when the days get long and the four walls begin to close in on us. No matter how many pressures or disappointments come into a person's life (and we've experienced plenty), you can't let them snuff out the joy—the precious gift of being alive.

I read an older novel recently by a woman named Elizabeth Goudge. One of the themes that emerged from its pages was that there are two fundamental ways to express love for God in this world. The first is obvious: love for our fellow man. The second isn't so obvious at all. She says that to express love for God, you need to express love for life. To love life, in other words, is really to love God. After all, God *is* life, the Creator and Sustainer of all living things. The author talks about waking up each morning "enchanted with the fact of being alive."

Now you may wake up in the morning not overly enchanted with much of anything—at least until you've had your coffee. But the truth remains that falling in love with life—staying excited about its adventures, mysteries, and possibilities—will enhance your love for God *and* your love for your spouse.

WHEN THE ROAD GETS ROUGH

Some of the best fireside stories for later years are not the ones where everything clicked along the tracks according to plan. Obviously, there are risky, uncomfortable, even frightening stretches of the road we walk together. Health crises, job crises, financial crises, parenting crises.

The most crucial priority is that these narrow places on the footpath drive you closer to each other—and closer to God—rather than pulling you apart.

Nanette: 🌿

Back in the early days of our marriage, I remember when we delivered a whole collection of Thom's artwork to a gallery in Southern California. With the last of our money, we'd decided to launch out and take a trip to Europe, trading one of Thom's paintings for the use of a friend's RV. We assumed, of course, that while we were gone his paintings would sell and we would have money when we got back.

But it didn't happen that way. For whatever reason, the paintings did not sell...and where in the world were we going to come up with our next mortgage payment? With no money at all, we had to brainstorm a plan to keep the Kinkade ship afloat for yet another month.

We put our heads together and came up with something. In the end, God provided for our needs, just as He always has, and we're still afloat after twenty years together. Looking back, we wouldn't trade those days of tramping around Europe together as a young, childless couple for any amount of money. And through that time of financial challenge, we learned to trust more in each other and trust more in our God to take care of us.

Back when we did the first prints of Thom's paintings, we once again had to literally put our very last dollar on the table, with no assurance that there would be a return. Neither of our families back home had much money, either, so we had no safety net beneath us for the plunge. We honestly didn't know what would happen. We didn't know what was around that bend in the road. But we had God and we had each other, so we took a deep breath and stepped out into space.

Yes, we could have put ourselves in a bit of trouble if things hadn't turned out. But we also put ourselves in a position to experience some of the happiest, most fulfilling moments of our lives as people around the country began recognizing Thom's gifts. We'd gone way out on a limb, but we found that the view was just fine from that vantage point. ❧

CERTAINLY, MARRIAGE ITSELF is a pathway that offers safety, comfort, and a measure of predictability. For one reason, there are two of you on the journey together. As Solomon wrote, "Two are better than one...if one falls down, his friend can help him up. But pity the man who falls and has no one to help him up!" (Ecclesiastes 4:9–10). Just being on a well-trod path assures you that other feet have been that way ahead of you, which is sometimes a comfort. But in any marriage, there will be those times when *nothing* looks familiar—times when the trail seems to vanish from beneath your feet.

I remember riding horseback about a year ago, climbing a hillside on what looked like a marvelous horse path. Heavy timber and granite outcroppings created a wall on my left. To my right, the ground fell away into a drop-off (of undetermined distance). It was a tight place, all right, but that trail seemed to be going somewhere—and was just wide enough for a climbing horse and an adventurous rider.

Then, as my horse and I came around yet another granite outcropping, we were confronted by a huge tree that had fallen straight across the path. *Now what?* At that point, we had no option but to forge our own way off into the brush—because there was no turning around on that trail!

That's where it began to get interesting. A low branch clawed the hat off my head, we skidded a bit on some loose rock, and I wondered if anyone would find this old artist's bones at the bottom of the canyon. Ever so carefully, my horse and I began to pick our way through the heavy shrubs on the downhill side of the tree.

That's when I encountered a pleasant surprise. What I

> *Sometimes, the very direction you've feared for years takes you to a place of beauty.*

had imagined was a sheer drop-off turned out to be more of a gentle slope. A little bit more riding brought us into a cathedral of huge, old-growth pines. The air was sweet and still, and I felt as though we'd entered some sort of sanctuary. The morning sun spilling through the pine boughs wove a golden tapestry on the forest floor.

Sitting there on my horse, I paused for a minute or two to breathe in the warmth and fragrance of that place before climbing back up to the trail. To me, that's such a poignant picture of our lives. The journey of discovery becomes priceless as you step off the beaten path and begin to experience God's alternate plan.

Sometimes, the very direction you've feared for years takes you to a place of beauty. Sometimes, the best pathway is no pathway at all.

When Nanette and I reminisce someday, I don't think we'll ever regret the times we took risks, plunged off the expected trail, and followed some of the wistful, winding roads that tugged at our hearts, for those were the times we felt closest! Sure, we've experienced our share of setbacks—and even a few minor disasters along the way. But even those incidents—frustrating or frightening at the time, perhaps—take on a bit of a glow when viewed through the long lens of memory.

At the very least, many years from now we won't be tapping our fingers on the table and staring blankly off into space as we sit together in a restaurant.

Forget the

profound,

momentous,

philosophical stuff.

Just talk.

CHAPTER FOUR

An Attentive Love

You wouldn't believe some of the gardens I've worked in over the last twenty years. I can close my eyes right now and see them…catching the first blush of a new day…languorous in the long light of a summer afternoon…yielding to gentle twilight shadows.

I've passed hour upon hour of joyous toil along winding dirt roads lined with split-rail fences. I've labored beside walls of sun-warmed brick and ornate gates of wrought iron, standing open to one and all. I've seen dew clinging to perfect yellow rosebuds and a white dogwood gilded with pale sunset gold. I've paused from my work on an afternoon so still you could hear a single bee at his labors. I've strolled winding cobbled paths with a practiced eye. I've lingered on stone bridges by lamplight, when fireflies dance along the gliding stream and mist gathers in the hollows. I've tended more flowers and fountains, bushes and trees, vines and trellises, than I can begin to number.

> *I've labored beside walls of sun-warmed brick and ornate gates of wrought iron, standing open to one and all.*

And here's the remarkable aspect of all this. Through it all, I've never wielded a spade, gripped a pair of shears, or wrapped my fingers around a single unyielding dandelion root.

All of my efforts have been accomplished with a brush, on canvas.

Though I have delighted in gardens on both sides

of the Atlantic, the ability to make such places blossom and thrive—to be part of the process—seems to elude me. I yield that skill to those who have the art of it in their fingers and the love of it in their blood.

Many of the gardens Nanette and I have fallen in love with are in England. The art of gardening, of course, is such a high part of English culture.

Nanette—with the aid of a few skilled professionals—does gardening around the Kinkade hacienda, bringing just a touch of an Old England summer to the flowerbeds of sunny California. She grew up in a family that always seemed to be dabbling with dirt and trowels and watering cans. As for me, I'm content to cheer them all on...from a safe distance on the sidelines, with a paintbrush in hand and a canvas at the ready. I'll savor the fragrance, bask in the beauty, and take great pleasure in the tranquil small worlds that other hands have created and maintain by the sweat of their brow, but the only foreign substance you're likely to find under *my* fingernails is paint.

Nanette: 🌿

During my growing-up years, gardening was our family's main hobby and recreation. No matter where we lived in the world, we always kept gardens. These days, with four girls to shepherd, I've reserved just a couple of small corners where I can still express a bit of creativity and get my fingers dirty now and then.

A true gardener, however, has to love the digging, weeding, hard labor, and meticulous care that goes into it. My parents—even now, in their later years—are constantly moving boulders, digging holes, attacking tree limbs with pruning shears, and even building rock walls. They're at it early in the morning and sometimes late into the evenings.

It's a reminder that all of that beauty and peace and lushness (as with most everything of value in life) comes with a price tag. 🌼

WHAT SOLOMON SAW

As I've painted so many serene, verdant gardens, as I've dipped my brush in a prism of a thousand seasonal hues, I've reflected on how much keeping a garden is like maintaining a happy marriage. The beauty of such places is a created beauty. It is a fragrant, pleasing place precisely because thoughtful, diligent people have made it so—and invest their lives to keep it so.

Just recently, I came across a passage in the book of Proverbs that speaks well to this need for diligence and care. It's a reminder to me of what can happen—to a garden, to a career, to a marriage, or to a walk with God—when vigilance gives way to apathy or neglect.

> I went past the field of the sluggard,
>   past the vineyard of the man who lacks judgment;
> thorns had come up everywhere,
>   the ground was covered with weeds,
>   and the stone wall was in ruins.
> I applied my heart to what I observed
>   and learned a lesson from what I saw:
> A little sleep, a little slumber,
>   a little folding of the hands to rest—

and poverty will come on you like a bandit
and scarcity like an armed man.

Solomon, of course, was a wide-eyed student of life and nature. Rather than lounging around his ivory palace eating grapes and watching acrobats and jugglers, he strapped on his hiking sandals and got out among his subjects on the hill-country trails and back roads of Israel. He took note of the ways of insects and animals, even getting down on his royal knees to observe the industry of an ant colony. He kept a trained eye on his orchards, fields, and vineyards and reflected on the habits and eccentricities of both men and women, kings and commoners.

In the passage above, I picture the son of David pausing by the roadside one afternoon to take note of a family manor in ruins. Most of us would have hurried right on by that rundown farm without a second glance, but Solomon found wisdom where others never seemed to look.

What was the story behind such a sad scene of decline and decay? This piece of property had once been someone's inheritance in Israel—one family's pride and precious possession since the days of Joshua. The field had fed generations and brought home good income. The vineyard had yielded good, sweet wine to be savored on days of feasting—or perhaps a dark winter evening. The stone wall had offered protection and privacy. And now?

Solomon had the kind of mind that was always asking why and how. Why had this collapse taken place? How had this small wedge of God's Promised Land fallen on such hard times?

He thought about it. Perhaps sitting on a rock or standing beside that crumbling wall, the great king took it all to heart.

> *I applied my heart to what I observed*
> *and learned a lesson from what I saw:*

And what did he learn?

> *A little sleep, a little slumber,*
> *a little folding of the hands to rest—*
> *and poverty will come on you like a bandit*
> *and scarcity like an armed man.*

PROVERBS 24:32–34

Decay occurs in small increments—with a devastating cumulative effect. When it comes to gardens, vineyards, and the relationship between a husband and wife, it doesn't take much neglect to bring poverty and loss to your own front door.

Nanette: 🌿

My parents would often remind me that the first rule of gardening is diligence. You just have to *be there*—every day—to water, to weed, to prune, to fertilize, to guard against invading armies of aphids, caterpillars, spider mites, snails, and a host of other relentless enemies. Without such vigilance, the only gardens anyone would ever see would be the two-dimensional kind in one of Thomas's paintings.

It's the same in a marriage. Unless you're watchful, actively cultivating the relationship, working at it with wide-open eyes and an attentive heart, it will begin to fall into ruin.

"Just a little sleep, a little slumber, a little folding of the hands..." In other words, it doesn't take

very long for a garden to go to seed. Just a little bit of compromise, a little bit of selfishness, a little bit of a ho-hum attitude, and that place of beauty and refuge begins to crumble right before your eyes. "Thorns everywhere...the ground covered with weeds...the stone wall in ruins." 🌼

MARRIAGE IS JUST AS much an action as a state of being. It's a *verb*, not just some sleepy noun that collects dust and rust. It's a consuming, ongoing activity; it is life itself.

I've had friends tell me, "Well, it's sad, but my marriage just fell apart." They speak as if it were something inevitable and unavoidable, as someone might say, "It rained last night" or "That last earthquake cracked our foundation."

But it isn't so. We are *not* passive victims of circumstance, no matter what our warped, self-absorbed culture may say. Could you imagine hearing a professional gardener sigh deeply and say something like this? "Well, you know, it's so unfortunate. But my garden—that little half-acre I've worked on for years—suddenly failed. I walked outside yesterday morning and—would you believe it? It was all overgrown. The place was chest-high with weeds, and aphids were chewing up everything in sight. It really gets me down."

And you would have to say, "Friend, where have you been? Was your garden really that important to you after all, or did you just tell yourself it was? Where have you been pouring your time? Where have you been devoting your energies and your creativity?" Beautiful gardens don't go to seed overnight, and neither do once-loving marriages. One of the many loves of marriage is a diligent, attentive love that refuses to ignore those little things that keep love in full bloom.

IT'S THE LITTLE THINGS

Someone once said that it's the little things that determine the big things. Just think of the daily maintenance that takes place on a Boeing 747. Little screws tightened. Little levers oiled. Little fuel lines checked. Little instruments calibrated. Why? Because if one or more of those small things is neglected, a jumbo-jet could suddenly fall out of the sky.

In the same way, small areas of neglect can do incalculable damage to a marriage. One researcher asks the question: "How does a couple get from a fight about washing dishes to legal arguments in divorce court? It's the snowball effect. When little things that couples fight about aren't properly dealt with, they can develop into larger problems. How couples manage the 'small stuff' may be a key factor in whether they achieve long-term conjugal bliss."[1]

I personally believe that the single most destructive potential in a marriage is simple lack of communication. Perhaps you've heard a man or woman complain, "The problem is we don't *really* communicate." And implicit in that comment are thoughts such as these: *We talk, but we don't connect at the deepest level. There's some kind of profound layer of verbal interaction that we keep missing.*

I don't mean to be uncharitable, but—I just don't buy that.

I believe communication in marriage is as simple as this: Raw hours together, looking in each other's eyes, your mouths moving. Forget "depth" of communication or "meaningful" talk. Forget the profound, momentous, philosophical stuff.

Just talk.

Talk every morning.

Talk every evening.

Talk on the phone during your lunch break.

Talk about everything and don't stop.

Why? Because marriage is all about *companionship*.

Nanette and I grow closer to each other just by discussing whether or not the kids should go to summer camp. We'll talk about the most trivial things you can imagine. She'll say, "Do you think Winsor is old enough to start wearing overalls?" We'll question each other on matters that might be considered minor or mundane on the surface, and yet…. A marriage is sewn together by ten thousand such tiny stitches. It's within the context of these little communications that we begin to work out the major issues of life.

And guess what? If you're daily working through those small questions, small irritants, small confessions and reconciliations, small joys, disappointments, and serendipities of life, it won't be so very difficult when the time comes to speak of weightier things. You'll move right into them in a natural, unpretentious way.

This is "time in the garden."

This is the sort of interaction that keeps a husband and wife linked and engaged with one another hour by hour, day by day.

Sure, maybe at some point we'll get to plunge into

some of those deep-end subjects about the nature of life. In fact, we had such a marathon conversation the last time we visited England. We walked along a little pathway by a stream at twilight, sat in the cool English clover, tossed pebbles into a quiet pool, and asked (and attempted to answer) some foundational questions. *Who are we? What are our big goals for the next phase of our lives? What will add to our happiness in the future? What changes do we need to make to keep our life simple and uncluttered?* This deep, soul-searching marathon of introspection must have lasted eight hours or more. (There must be something in the rarified air of a rural British village that inspires such talk.) But for the most part, Nanette and I simply enjoy each other's companionship day by day in the sometimes mundane give-and-take of life on an imperfect planet.

This woman is my other half. Why should I make a half-witted decision by myself?

I know that some couples tend to strictly categorize duties and responsibilities in their marriage. "You handle this; I'll handle that. You manage the house; I'll manage the car. You talk to our kids; I'll talk to our broker. You pay the bills; I'll handle the social calendar."

But Nanette Kinkade is one wife who likes to have her husband's input on anything and everything—and I want hers, too. I've heard some guys say, "My wife picks out the bedspreads and chooses the paint for the hallway. It doesn't matter to me. I leave all the decorating to her." That's a workable model, I suppose, but it's never been that way in our home.

Nanette doesn't *want* to buy the bedspread until she's talked to me about the options. We enjoy inter-acting about those minor, nitty-gritty details of our life together. It isn't a burden or a hassle; it's a delight. And by the same token, I wouldn't want to finish a painting without seeing it through her eyes. I wouldn't want to make a business decision without gaining her perspective. After all, this woman is my other half. Why should I make a half-witted decision by myself? I treasure her input. It's one of my bellwethers that I've come to depend on in our ventures. If Nanette gets excited about something and really agrees with the direction, then I'm strapping on my seat belt, getting ready to launch.

Nanette:

Married life truly is a mosaic of *little* things. Little touches. Little words. Little smiles of encouragement. Little expressions of endearment.

As my parents could tell you, it only takes a little neglect, here and there, to ruin a lovely garden. Familiarity with one another can lead us to be sloppy in our behavior and in our conversation, sometimes treating our spouse in a way that we would never treat a friend or business associate. Even when we're relaxed at home with loved ones, we still need to be very careful to think before we speak and to consider before we act. It doesn't take a major case of abuse or infidelity to destroy the garden of marriage. It can be the cumulative effect of all those little things we have left untended: all the weeds left unpulled. All the flowers left unwatered. All the pests left to do their damage. Inch by inch, the garden withers and dies.

GOD CREATED ALL OF US WITH certain basic needs. I need to be affirmed in my creative work. That's a big identity point to me. I don't seem to need a whole lot of praise for my physical appearance, my taste in clothing, or my effectiveness in business. But it means everything to me to feel like I'm reaching someone through my paintings. Nanette understands that, of course, and is careful to provide that sort of input. She's always attentive when I want to enthuse about new techniques or fresh ideas. Actually, I'm one of those people who constantly bubbles over with myriad new ideas. And even though she knows very well that less than one in ten will ever go anywhere, Nanette is always there to listen, ask questions, and get excited with me. She isn't just nodding her head up and down and thinking of something else. She's really *with* me in these things.

On her side of things, Nanette has a deep need for security within the relationship. She wants to feel that I'm taking care of myself, that I'm watching my health, and that I'll be there for the long haul. She wants to be assured that I'm really aware of the needs of the kids. As a husband, I know I can love my spouse by creatively paying attention to my children. This factor may well be (especially for the husband) one of the most neglected tools to strengthen a marriage. You will touch her heart by showing her that you're a committed dad, by planning fun activities for the family, and by really taking the time to think through how you might bless your kids every day.

SMALL GESTURES

Nanette: 🌿

There's such a variety of little things that we can do for each other. One morning recently, for instance, Thom said, "Honey, why don't I take the girls to school today?" We had just gotten back from a trip the night before, we were all tired, and I had my hands full trying to catch up on things at home. So Thom took time away from his studio (even though I know he loves to get an early start) to drive Winsor and Evie to school. That saved about an hour of my time. It was a little gesture—a small sacrifice—that meant so much to me. He offered his time because he knew I was weary and that the tasks were stacking up for me. (And also because he loves communicating with the little ones during the drive to school.)

He's always doing little things like that. He'll make tea over in his studio and call me. "I just made tea. Do you want to come over and have a cup with me?" Or "Let's take our lunch and go sit out on the lawn." Yes, you might call some of those gestures insignificant. Hardly worth mentioning. But who can calculate their cumulative impact on a marriage?

If we would just stay *tuned in* to one another's needs, we would find that so many old hurts and understandings begin to melt away, never to return. 🌸

WHEN NEGLECT SETS IN

Nanette and I used to spend time with a certain couple we knew from Placerville, but we haven't seen them in years. Frankly, our relationship with this couple was becoming a little uncomfortable.

I love paying attention to my wife, complimenting her, and telling her how attractive she looks. We'd be out somewhere with this couple, and I'd say something to Nanette like, "Wow, honey, you look incredible tonight!" And this other woman would glare at her husband, slug him on the arm, and say, "*See?* How come you never say that kind of stuff to *me?*"

At first it was mildly funny. But as time went on, it became more and more awkward. I couldn't be my normal self because this other woman was so obviously envious of the way I treated Nanette. After a while, it became all too clear that this man just wasn't giving his wife any attention. And when she saw what that kind of care and attentive love looked like—when she saw that

> *I love paying attention to my wife, complimenting her, and telling her how attractive she looks.*

a man could be that courteous to his wife—she began craving the same treatment from her husband. I felt like shaking this guy by the shoulders and saying, "Praising your spouse is not that difficult to do! Don't you get it?"

To tell the truth, I don't know if he'll ever "get it." Or even if he does, if he'll ever take it to heart. If Solomon had been looking over the garden wall of this man's marriage, he would have seen wilted foliage...and the persistent march of nettles and weeds.

Nanette: ❧

A dear friend of mine has always made me think of a neglected garden. Life with her husband has been very difficult. I really admire her character and personal strength to stay with the relationship and to give her best to it—even though she feels like she's dying inside sometimes.

For her part, she works very hard to see the good in her husband, magnify those things, and really praise him and build him up. As she practices these disciplines, the relationship improves—a little. The problem is, she never gets much of it back! She feels so neglected, so uncared for. Her heart is like a garden that's been given no attention and no water—for years. So what do you end up with? Weeds and barrenness.

The ironic thing is that this man is a good financial provider and has always been faithful. But it's as if he has no concept of a woman's emotional needs. He seems incapable of giving her any appreciation, admiration, or those little signs of love that mean so much to a woman.

She keeps hoping and hoping that someday—as she extends love and appreciation to him—it will "catch." And perhaps (with such loving persistence and by God's grace) it will.

Being with her, however, makes me value my husband all the more. He's so appreciative and takes every opportunity to give me honor and praise.

I don't ever want to take that for granted. ❧

WORTH IT ALL

In the old children's classic *The Secret Garden*, a lonely orphan girl named Mary Lennox discovers a locked and forsaken garden on the estate of her reclusive uncle and guardian. With tender care and daily diligence, that small, desolate place behind the high walls becomes a sanctuary, full of life, color, song, and peace.

For Nanette and me, our marriage has always been that secret garden: a peaceful, fragrant place, a refuge from the hurts and hassles of an indifferent world. For us, "working the garden" means building each other up, accepting each other unconditionally, making small sacrifices for each other, praying daily for each other, and taking care to attend to each other's needs—whether emotional, sexual, or spiritual.

Best of all, we meet our Lord in that garden place. He's the Master Gardener who shows us where to weed, when to prune, and how to guard against those enemies—great and small—that might rob our garden of beauty and sap away its life.

It demands a great deal of work.

In fact, it will demand your very life.

But when you find yourself walking in that garden some cool morning, when you're inhaling that fragrance and letting the peace wash across you like a soft summer wind, you will know in your heart that all the time and work has been worthwhile.

---

1. Dr. Marc Schulz, "'It's the Little Things...' Forgiveness and Long-Term Marriage" (research project, Bryn Mawr College, Pennsylvania, n.d.).

Marriage is
all about building
bridges and
spanning canyons.

CHAPTER FIVE

A Sharing Love

Nanette: 🌿

We came upon the old bridge just before sunset. We'd been rambling along a narrow footpath, following a bend in the stream.

Suddenly, there it was. A small, gray, stone arch over the dark, gliding water. Weathered and worn, it might well have been there for centuries. But the years hadn't diminished its simple grace and beauty.

One sidelong glance told me what my husband was thinking. His eyes shone with that speculative glow I've seen so many times. He was already seeing visions and dreaming dreams. He was pondering perspective and depth, light and shadow, palette and texture. There was no doubt about it; that elegant little bridge—now bathed in the soft light of an English sunset—would one day be a Thomas Kinkade painting, gracing millions of homes around the world.

Our adventure began over ten years ago, when we gathered up suitcases, paints, and little girls and retreated halfway across the world to Fairford, a small village in rural England. We rented a small cottage with no TV or telephone and stayed there for two months.

It was one of the best times of our lives.

Back home, our business was just mushrooming. That was the good news. The bad news was that our little enterprise really wasn't big enough to hire the help we needed. As a result, we tried to cover all the bases ourselves. Thom had felt himself increasingly distracted from his painting by all the pressures, logistics, phone calls, and opportunities.

As exciting as it was to see Thom's recognition and popularity building across the country, something about that situation didn't ring true. How could we allow success and growing demands to draw Thom away from the very pursuit that created that success? How could he go on creating worlds of tranquility and peace on canvas when he was being pulled seventeen different ways from morning till night?

The business, we decided, would just have to wait. (And, thank the Lord, it did.) Thom felt an urgency to get away from the intensity for a while to pursue his true calling: creating works of art for the glory of God.

In merry old England there were no interruptions, no time-robbing phone calls, no faxes, no interview requests, and no demands to divert Thom from his easel. He painted every day, hour upon joyful hour, and we all basked in the slower pace.

Evidently, the principal recreation for the

townspeople of Fairford during those summer evenings was walking. Everyone, young and old, seemed to turn out at day's end for extended strolls, and the Kinkades gladly fell into that rhythm. We had two little ones at that time: Merritt was three, and Chandler was about five months.

The pleasant thing about England—a nation with a long tradition of walking tours (or "rambles," as the English call them)—is that you can wander just about anywhere you please without fear of trespassing. There are few restrictions about crossing private property if you're on a footpath to somewhere else. So every evening, little ones in tow, we would go exploring, often following the path by the stream that wound its way through the village and into the twilight fields beyond.

On one such jaunt, we discovered the bridge. For the next four or five afternoons to follow, we returned to the foot of that bridge with a large picnic basket and a few favorite toys. The girls and I relaxed and played and napped by the stream, while Thom captured the scene on canvas. He titled that painting "Broad Water Bridge," and it became one of the most successful of our early releases. ❧

THERE'S SOMETHING ABOUT BRIDGES...

Bridges have always stirred my imagination in some deep and inexplicable way. Bridges are a transition point from one sphere of existence to another. Bridges help us span the obstacles life places before us. If we find ourselves facing a rushing river, we're either going to get very wet and risk a drowning, or we're going to build a bridge. If we're confronted by a deep canyon with sheer rocky walls, we're either going to borrow some ropes and climbing equipment, or we're going to build a bridge.

> *In Christ, we share the same eternal destiny.*

Marriage is all about building bridges and spanning canyons. In fact, you might say that married life is *lived* on a bridge.

As man and woman, we are two distinct countries separated by our genders, personalities, backgrounds, perspectives, preferences, and peculiarities. We each possess our own hopes, dreams, dreads, and fears. Yet in marriage, those two countries become one, united under a single flag, issuing a single currency, and joined by a permanent bridge. You might picture a wedding as a ribbon-cutting ceremony, opening that bridge from heart to heart, soul to soul. Yes, we're still individuals. But now, in the eyes of heaven, we are "one nation, under God." We're a *unit*—two against the world!—linked by our love, by our physical union, and by our solemn vows.

As a consequence, traffic in those bridge lanes needs to be wide open. It's a span that must have free access at all times (with no tolls to pay), so that the love and help, friendship and companionship, esteem and perspective, can flow unimpeded.

By focusing on the bridge itself, we can understand that each person's individual uniqueness doesn't end just because we have become one. In marriage we have a chance to celebrate those uniquenesses while standing on the bridge together.

In recent days, our culture has bought into the pop psychology trend that says men and women are so radically different, so utterly alien to one another, that there is little common ground for communication. After all, how do you build a bridge all the way from Mars to Venus?

That is certainly neither God's perspective nor His plan. Without criticizing what might be a helpful metaphor in some ways, I must say that in reality, men and women are not from different planets. All humans, regardless of their gender, were made in the image of the same Creator and redeemed by the same Lord. We are eternally bound together on the same world with the same needs, albeit expressed in different ways. In Christ, we share the same eternal destiny. Separately, we reflect human diversity in its loveliest form; together, we have the potential for wondrous parallel interaction, integrating two halves of humanity—separated at Creation—into a harmonized whole.

A WIDER VIEW

A few years ago, I took a big step back from painting small-town covered bridges and graceful stone bridges in sleepy countryside settings.

That was the year I took on the Golden Gate.

As a result, I found myself squinting across San Francisco Bay at a Herculean 894,500-ton structure composed of basically two elements: concrete and steel. The bridge we call marriage, however, is composed of many elements—some fragile, some incredibly strong. These include commitment, communication, dedication, loyalty, mutual respect, esteem, and shared interests, to name just a few.

To me, a bridge is a marvel, a work of art in a category of its own. I've often thought that people seem blind to the beauty of these structures all around us. We speed over them on our journeys or cross them daily on our commutes without a second thought. But a bridge is so much more than a mere transportation link; it is a wonder in and of itself. Through the years, I have developed the somewhat dangerous habit of stopping my car in the middle of a bridge (if I don't see another car immediately behind me). If you happen to see me climb out of my car to stare over the rail, don't call 911 on your cell phone. Jumping is the furthest thing from my mind. I just like to absorb the view.

> *The moonlight turned the wide waters into a vast silver highway.*

Before I was married, another art student and I tucked our sketchbooks into backpacks and set off to be hoboes for a summer, hopping freight trains and hitchhiking from coast to coast. I'll never forget the humid, moonlit night we crossed the Mississippi. My buddy and I were lounging comfortably on top of an open carload of sweet-smelling pine chips on their way to a paper mill somewhere in Dixie.

Suddenly we found ourselves on a massive trestle, with the great river rolling beneath us. The moonlight turned the wide waters into a vast silver highway, plied by tugs towing trains of barges. I would have given anything for my paints at that moment—and the ability to stop the train right there on the tracks. But all too soon we rumbled on through the dark Mississippi delta and the moment was gone. To this day, the fragrance of pine takes me back to that summer night on the long bridge, rolling across the Father of Waters.

A bridge, you see, is a place of contemplation and perspective. It is not only a place of transit, but also of elevation—and even *revelation*. From a bridge, you can often see great distances—farther than you can see from the road at either approach. The highway itself might be a series of curves surrounded by a wall of foliage, trees, or forest. But from a bridge, you can see out and beyond the obstacles. You can see a different direction. You gain a wider view.

Nanette: 🌿

When you stand on a bridge, you have a feeling that you've overcome something. There may be rushing water down below, but you are walking *over* it. There may be great distances or hidden perils beneath your feet, but you are in a safe place, up above the canyons and empty places.

Relational bridges do that for us, too. They lift us up above those fears and burdens each of us carries and bring us to a safe place of coming together—a place where we share our worries and concerns with one another and find our load lightened. Bridges in marriage are those things that bind you together day by day: communication, compliments, understanding, support, fun, laughter, experiences (both good and bad), overcoming challenges together, children, regular sexual expression, time together, shared faith, and prayer. 🌺

I CAN THINK OF SO MANY times in our marriage when my perspective clamped down around me, and I couldn't see farther than the end of my nose. Again and again, Nanette had just the right word or insight for me that challenged me to trust in God, or helped me take a wider, longer view. And it's been true for her as well. Together, our perspective has seemed far wider than the sum of two individuals. The Lord has revealed things to us as a couple as we've opened our hearts to one another.

THE BRIDGE OF ESTEEM

As a young, unknown, penniless artist, I lived with a chip on my shoulder. Unfailingly, whenever I walked through an art gallery with Nanette, I would find myself becoming frustrated and angry.

I would look at those paintings on the wall and think, *My work is as good as this—maybe even better. Why can't I get a showing? How come I can't get anywhere? Why can't I get a break?* When the owners of the gallery would speak to me, I'd find myself snapping at them. "Why are you showing this artist?" I know it must have been uncomfortable for Nanette sometimes.

Part of it, of course, was simple immaturity.

Twenty-four years old and newly married, I was really just getting started. Even so, I felt insecure about my future and wanted desperately to prove myself. As a result, I became increasingly antagonistic and cynical toward the art community. My perspective seemed to shrink as my discouragement grew.

But Nanette just kept esteeming me.

"Honey," she would say, "your art *is* better. You know it is. God has gifted you in a special way, and He's going to use you. You'll see! You just have to trust Him and wait on Him."

Nanette coaxed me out of my disappointment and isolation and onto the bridge of esteem. Out there on that high and lofty span beside her, I would regain some of my lost perspective. I'd calm myself down, glue myself back together, and go back to my easel day after day and work as hard as I could. Instead of wasting my energy resenting those who "get all the breaks," I poured myself into each painting and persevered.

Looking back, I realize now what a dangerous time it was for me—both personally and professionally. Since those days, I've encountered this solemn warning in the book of Hebrews: "See to it that no one comes short of the grace of God; that no root of bitterness springing up causes trouble, and by it many be defiled" (Hebrews 12:15, NASB).

I *was* coming short of God's grace and kindness through my impatience and anger—and found myself in danger of becoming a bitter young man. Satan could have used that time in my life to end my career before it had a chance to begin. I could have given myself over to a life-sapping cynicism and sunk into a "poor me" mind-set that might have stretched on for years. I could have easily told myself, "Aw, some artists will always get preferential treatment—the guys with the connections or the rich friends. So why should I work my tail off at this? Nobody's going to pay attention to a poor artist from a dinky town like Placerville. I may as well shelve this and get a day job."

If she still had faith in me, maybe I could scrape together enough faith in myself to stick with our dreams.

It could have happened. But it *didn't* happen because Nanette Kinkade built a bridge of esteem into my life. In her quiet, gentle way, she kept telling me again and again, "You *are* worthwhile, Thomas. No one paints quite like you do. You haven't been noticed yet by some of the galleries, but you need to keep working because your art is wonderful. I have faith in you."

This was the same girl who had believed in me when I was a thirteen-year-old neighbor boy from a broken home, full of dreams and crazy ideas. If she still had faith in me, maybe I could scrape together enough faith in myself to stick with our dreams.

That esteem, that wider perspective, enabled me to put the worries and anger aside so that I could just flat work hard during that season of my life. And sure enough, just as Nanette had said, the recognition and success began to trickle in. And then it began to snowball.

Just a year or two later, I had the privilege of returning the favor. Soon after we had Merritt, our first child, Nanette entered a season where she lost all confidence in her ability as a mom. Doubts and fears flooded her mind and played havoc with her emotions. Her feelings of self-worth plunged through the floor, and she convinced herself that she would *never* be a good mother, that she would *never* be able to handle all the demands.

As it had been with me a few years earlier, it was a

time when Satan could have harmed her, crippling her emotions and all her wonderful potential. My role and my desire in those days was simply to keep doing for her what she had so consistently done for me.

"Nanette, please listen to me. You're doing just fine. This time of stress—it's just a tunnel. We're going to get through it together—out into the light. You'll see! You're a super wife, you're going to be a super mom, and I'm just really proud of you. I'm praying for you, and I know God is going to help you to be the best you can be."

From time to time through the years, the doubts have edged back in, and I've always tried to be a rock for her, whatever the issue that might be troubling her. "Honey, that school we picked for the girls is going to work out just fine" or "This decision you're making about the kids' camp this summer will be great for them—and for the whole family." Those seemingly small choices and decisions can absolutely undermine her confidence and steal her joy.

So we meet each other in the middle of that bridge called Esteem and find perspective and strength to walk hand in hand into each new day.

INCLUDING EACH OTHER

Nanette:

Thom and I have always made it a priority to take time for each other. After we get our children to bed and there is quiet in the house, we set everything else aside just to be together and talk, to share our day, and to encourage each other. We've often said to each other, "I could never leave you because I'd lose my best friend!"

It has meant so much to me that Thom has wanted to include me in his career. He's made me a part of every phase—right from the beginning when we were stretching canvases in our tiny living room and spending our weekends at one-man shows in shopping malls and outdoor markets. Because Thom has been so careful and consistent to include me, we now feel that this ministry is *ours* together, something we've built as a team. I know very well that it's Thom's art and that he's the one with the special artistic gifting, but he's made me feel so much a part of it all. He seeks my opinion on each painting, shares his ideas and concerns with me, and brings his excitement home at night when the Lord has given him a good painting day. Even little things like hiding my initial in his paintings (the famous hidden N) through the years have made me feel like I have an integral stake in his life and ministry.

I really have no background in art, and I've never considered myself artistically inclined. But I like to have my own set of paints and to paint with

> *Find something that you both enjoy and can do together so that you can continue to build those bridges through the years.*

Thomas when we're in some inspiring setting together. The truth is, I *want* to be involved in my husband's career—because I want to be involved with my husband! If he's painting for hours on end, I want to be with him doing the same thing, when time allows.

I would encourage any couple, new or old, to find common interests and *pursue* them—especially if it can involve each other's careers.

Overcome those inevitable objections and obstacles and find something that you both enjoy and can do together so that you can continue to build those bridges through the years.

I can honestly say that I've never felt any lack of self-esteem in supporting Thom's career rather than building my own. I know that sort of statement flies in the face of our contemporary culture and mind-set—but what a strong bridge it builds between husband and wife! I have seen so many marriages where two busy career people have spun off in separate directions and have no time at all for one another. And then when crises come (as they will), they have no bridges between them, no common ground. They find themselves trying to communicate across a gulf—shouting from opposite banks of a wide river—and in despair because they can't make themselves heard or understood. ❀

A FEW YEARS AGO, Nanette and I took up the game of golf together. If she hadn't been interested, I might never have pursued it. Ultimately, I viewed it as a way to build a highway of shared experiences out into our future. After all, golf is a game you can do in your old age—a little more feebly, perhaps, but you can still do it.

The golf club we now belong to has some delightful couples in their eighties and nineties—some real characters who keep us in stitches in the clubhouse. I had no real interest in golf ten years ago, until I began to see it as an expression of everything I love: the beauty of nature, the serenity of peaceful settings, and (best of all) time with Nanette, my best friend. Throw some moderate exercise into the mix, and how can you go wrong?

When I first approached Nanette with the idea, she admitted that it wasn't something she would have normally considered. But adventurous lady that she is, she agreed to give it a try. We took a few lessons, and now we really look forward to our times together on the course. Neither of us is very good—and may never get a whole lot better—but we just view it as a way to build memories together for the rest of our lives.

Golf, by the way, doesn't have to be an expensive hobby. You can pick up clubs at a garage sale, and just about anyone can afford to play at a local municipal golf course.

But maybe your interests and inclinations as a couple

would lead you in a completely different direction. Riding horses or rockhounding, backpacking or fishing, skiing or operagoing, or hitting garage sales every Saturday. The point is, find something you can do *together*. Meet halfway on that bridge and treasure those hours together, instead of choosing separate activities that will end up dividing rather than uniting you.

A BRIDGE TO THE FUTURE

Nanette and I are champions at planning phases of life. We're always strategizing "the next phase," recognizing, of course, that it's all subject to God's grace and will. But even with four children at home right now, we're looking forward to the phase when it will just be the two of us, with no kids at home. That's still fifteen years or so away, but the way we see it, if you don't think about these things ahead of time, you won't build up anticipation and you will miss so much of the enjoyment of life that might have been possible.

Just recently, I've been thinking ahead to grandkids. I've got plans in mind for annual traditions that could involve our children and grandchildren, should God bless us in that way. That's a long way off. Grandpa Thom and Grandma Nanette are still over the horizon somewhere. But when you're standing on the bridge together, you can see things in the distance you would never see if you were alone on some highway winding through the woods.

Nanette and I love to plan and build dreams together. We're weaving two strands of dreams into one stronger rope that will bind us closer together with each passing year.

After all, we're going to be husband and wife for the rest of our lives. We accept no other option or possibility. That being so, we're working side by side to build a bridge into a future we cannot see. Obviously, no one knows what the next day—or even the next hour—might bring. But as long as God gives us life, we can count on being together. And we can count on the strong, guiding hand of our Great Shepherd, who has been to the future ahead of us and will show us the way.

If you've never followed a whim...well, who knows what you may have missed!

CHAPTER SIX

A Spontaneous Love

Experiences are better than any movie you've ever seen.

Experiences are better than any novel you've ever read.

Experiences are better than any computer game you've ever played.

Why? Because they're *yours*. And the memories you carry with you will become a family inheritance beyond anything money can buy.

Experiences are more to be sought after and treasured than any material possession you could ever own. From the time we were kids—bouncing on the trampoline in her backyard—Nanette and I decided that we would be people who experience *real* life. Come Hades or High Water, whether or not we ever had any money (and for much of our lives we had very little), we were going to get out there and taste as much of life together as we could.

I've come to the conclusion that there are two types of people: those who truly experience life and those who content themselves with vicarious, artificial "experiences" through the entertainment-media monolith of our culture.

It comes down to this: You can tune into a history show, or you can go out and make a little history of your own. You can watch a learning network, or you can break out of the box and get your learning firsthand. You can click on a cable channel dedicated to adventure and discovery, or you can set forth from your four walls to discover life in all its wonder and awesome beauty. You can watch innumerable movie channels with ever bigger screens and ever more realistic sound systems, or you can escape your couch and your remote, take your spouse by the hand, and *live* some adventures that have never been manufactured in a Hollywood studio—adventures you'll be recalling together (and perhaps regaling your grandchildren) years and years from now.

Life on this planet! It's fragile. It's precious. It's incredibly brief, and it's coming to a home and marriage near you. Just open your eyes in the morning, stretch those confining comfort zones (otherwise known as "ruts"), and begin to experience it together.

> *You can tune into a history show, or you can go out and make a little history of your own.*

You have to do a bit of planning, of course, if you're going to get time away from the routine and the pressures to try something new. For this reason, over the years Nanette and I have planned trips, bike rides, camping excursions, and long country rambles. But after you've made your basic plans, you also need to leave room—in fact, lots of room—for spontaneity.

And if you've never followed a whim…well, who knows what you may have missed!

CHASING A FAIRY-TALE VISION

For some reason, the little painting on the third shelf seemed to call to me.

It really wasn't much of a painting. Some unknown artist of dubious skill had sought to capture the idyllic scene back in the 1920s. It wasn't the art that intrigued me. It was what it portrayed: a village nestled in a little valley, surrounded by soaring mountain peaks. Stunning. But was it real—or simply a scene out of the artist's imagination?

I had a hunch it was real. And if it existed, I wanted to go there.

I beckoned to the dealer of the antique store, his gloomy countenance brightening at the prospect of a sale. (Apparently that little painting had been occupying the third shelf for quite some time.) I pointed to the picture and attempted a question in my broken, phrase-book German.

"Where is this?"

"Heiligenblut."

"Excuse me?"

"Heiligenblut."

If I wasn't mistaken, he'd just said "holy blood." Twice. But what in the world did he mean? He kept pointing at the picture until I finally got the idea. Heiligenblut was the name of the village.

Suddenly I was elated. This place *was* real. And from the mountains portrayed in the painting, it appeared to be in the Alps…which happened to be where we were, too.

Through a series of clumsy interchanges, I learned that Heiligenblut was an Austrian village on the other side of the Alps from where we were, but not so very far away as the crow flew. (But what if the crow had to drive a rented car? How far would it be then?) The village, he told me, was something of a landmark for Austrians, but was rarely visited by tourists.

Well, that settled it. We were going. We just had to make a pilgrimage to that gingerbread village in the mountain valley with the remarkable name.

Much to the shopkeeper's chagrin, I left the little painting right where it was, on the third shelf.

I wanted to experience the real thing.

"YOU WANT TO GO *WHERE?*"

Nanette and I were traveling with another couple in Europe. We'd booked a hotel in Salzburg but had nothing else on our itinerary for a few days other than poking around some of the shops.

Our friends were more than ready for some quiet R and R.

The Kinkades were more than ready for adventure.

> *If you turned away at the prospect of every risk, you'd never go anywhere.*

When we announced our intention to set off on a pilgrimage to Heiligenblut the next day, our friends couldn't believe it. ("Let me get this straight, Thom. You saw a village in an old painting in an antique shop—and now you want to go *find* it?") They immediately ran all the standard objections up the flagpole: *What if we get lost? What if this place is different from the picture? What if we can't find a place to stay? How do we know this won't be a waste of time?*

Obstacles of that sort always loom in the path of true adventure. (Can you imagine the conversations Columbus must have had with his mother before he set sail?) If you turned away at the prospect of every risk, you'd never go anywhere. You'd end up like that voiceless elderly couple in the restaurant I mentioned earlier in the book: eating a full dinner in utter silence, with nothing left to talk about.

I finally persuaded our friends to join us, reluctant as they were. With a little help from the locals, we obtained a map of our course and set off the next morning for soaring adventure in the high Alps.

It was a happy moment when we actually saw Heiligenblut on a road sign, pointing off toward the mountains. There couldn't be many towns with *that* name. According to the map, however, the village was on the other side of the mountains. How in the world were we going to get across those daunting peaks— especially with the threat of snow in the air?

By then, of course, we were caught up in the thrill of the hunt. No paltry obstacles (like the Alps) were going to get in our way now. We set off on the little winding road up onto the shoulders of the great mountains.

A little farther up, Nanette exclaimed, "Look up there!" She pointed excitedly toward one of the slopes. "It looks like the road goes into a tunnel."

A tunnel? That made sense. But instead of driving straight into that yawning darkness as we anticipated, the road abruptly petered out in a gravel parking lot at what looked like a train station.

Now what? Between the four of us, we knew enough German to ask a few people how to get to Heiligenblut. They looked at us with that condescending, how-could-you-not-know-this? expression and indicated that we would have to go on the railway cars just like everyone else.

Our friends had misgivings, but that was nothing new. Anyway, you can't live your life under the shadow of others' apprehensions and expectations. This was shaping up to be a first-class memory maker, and I intended to relish every moment.

We had coffee in the station's little café, watching a flurry of snow sweep across the valley and begin to cloak the platform. The train, pulled by a big, noisy steam engine, announced its presence miles before it reached the station. But then we were in for another surprise. There were no passenger cars. This was a train of flatcars.

Suddenly the parking lot seemed overflowing with cars—all waiting to drive up a series of hastily assembled ramps onto the flatcars themselves. "How about that?" I thought to myself. "A train ride through the mountains in the comfort of your own car!"

On the map, the tunnel appeared to be over thirty miles long. Once inside, we realized our journey would be without the benefit of light. For the next forty-five minutes, we would be racing along (backward, it turned out) at sixty miles an hour through the dark heart of Europe's most formidable mountains.

What a remarkable escapade! And to think it all began with a spontaneous conversation in an antique shop!

About forty-five minutes later we pulled out of the tunnel, squinting at the light. Heiligenblut turned out to be the most delightful, picturesque village we had ever encountered in the Alps. It looked as though it had sprung up from the pages of Grimm's fairy tales and seemed populated by a friendly group of Austrian mountain folk right out of central casting.

From a vantage point on an Alpine mountainside, I got out my paints and did a quick plein air study of the village in the valley. But even without the painting, our memories will always be sharp and clear—bringing a smile to our faces to this day.

We took a chance, and we were rewarded with a serendipity.

A BIT OF A RISK

We never saw Heiligenblut on any brochure. It wasn't a part of anybody's package tour, and we'd never read about it in the pages of a travel magazine. All we had to go on was an eighty-year-old painting and the word of a disappointed antique dealer.

We had seen a road sign and followed it, not really knowing where we were going or how we were going to get there. The journey simply unfolded before us as we traveled. And the joy of discovery is something Nanette and I will still be talking about when we're hobbling across the golf course in our nineties.

That's the blessing of spontaneity.

And that's what helps keep life exciting and a marriage fresh and fun.

As much as Nanette and I applaud the value of planning adventures and outings (anticipation is half the fun), we also like to leave room for unplanned experiences along the way. In fact, if you plan everything ahead of time, you'll often feel let down: The hotel won't be as nice as the brochure described it; the "charming" village will turn out to be a tacky tourist trap.

Sometimes it's more fun to just launch out and discover as you go, taking the good with the bad, the wide-open vistas along with the bumpy dead ends. How can you be "let down" if you haven't front-loaded the trip with high expectations? But if you're approaching it all with a spirit of adventure and exploration, you will often be rewarded by an experience you never could have planned or scheduled.

The great thing about stepping out of the realm of the predictable and the expected is the mutual exhilaration it provides...and the indelible memories it prints in your mind.

> *The journey simply unfolded before us as we traveled.*

One of the worship songs we often sing in our church contains the words: *Our God is the God of happenstance, He is Master of every circumstance....*

If you truly believe that God is in control of life, then there are no random meetings or conversations or encounters. Each day offers wondrous opportunities disguised as common events. An adventure might begin with the chance meeting of an old friend, a comment overheard from a stranger, or even an intriguing thought that we wake up with. Who knows where such seemingly insignificant forks in the path might lead? We can expect that God's plan will yield unexpected twists and turns, with discoveries, lessons, stern challenges, and blessings all along the way.

Every morning I open my eyes and say, "God, thank You for another day—another chance to be alive and to see You work in my life. Lord, You know I'm far from perfect. Miles from where I could be or should be. You know (better than anyone else) how far I have to go to be the person You want me to be. But here I am, Lord. The sun's up. The coffee's brewing. I'm alive, I'm healthy. I'm dependent on You for everything. What do You have for me today? I'm ready for it. Whatever comes my way, guide me in Your wisdom, sustain me by Your strength, comfort me by Your kindness, and lead me by Your grace."

Nanette: 🌿

There are so many parallels between a marriage and a person's relationship with the Lord. Spontaneity in either relationship grows out of trust. Since I trust Thom, feel secure in my relationship with him, and know that he loves and esteems me, I'm not afraid to take risks with him, to try new things and brave new experiences. No matter what happens, I know that we'll still have each other, and that's what matters most.

It's the same in our walk with God. If our trust is in Him, we can rise above our feelings of insecurity and fear, knowing that He will guide us, care for us, and work all of life's events together for our ultimate good.

Some people have planned their lives so meticulously that they leave no room for the Holy Spirit to direct them— to turn them in one direction or another by His "still, small voice." There's a verse in the book of Isaiah that says, "Whether you turn to the right or to the left, your ears will hear a voice behind you, saying, 'This is the way; walk in it'" (Isaiah 30:21). That's a beautiful way to live. But I think some of us would want to argue with God at that point and say, "Yes, Lord, but it doesn't fit into my *plans!*"

Someone once said, "Blessed are the flexible, for they shall not be broken." How true that is!

Those who hold life loosely, trusting God and yielding to His direction, will never be crushed by unexpected circumstances or changes in fortune. Living in a more spontaneous way forces you to be more dependent on God and, in a marriage relationship, to grow in your trust for one another. As you walk through challenging— even frightening—experiences together, you find yourself drawing closer, developing a bond that might never have happened otherwise. ❧

ARE PLANNING AND SPONTANEITY OPPOSITES?

There is a balance, of course, between planning and spontaneity. You sketch out the big plan and the major direction, but you leave room for discovery, for adventure, and for the unexpected. For example, you may know that you are going to Paris and where you intend to stay, but out on a walk one fine morning you might strike up a conversation with a street musician who ends up showing you a little Bohemian café—far from the haunts of the average tourist—where you have lunch. This exact thing has happened to Nanette and me.

People who overschedule such trips, rigidly planning every five-minute block, are going to miss the surprises, the serendipities, and the Heiligenbluts along the way.

Nanette and I are planning a trip to Europe in the near future in which we've determined to make *no* arrangements. Frankly, we don't know where we'll be staying. We don't know where we'll be dining. We don't know where we'll spend our time. We're going to pick up a

> *All it takes is a little spontaneity, a little willingness to flex.*

rental car in Amsterdam, and then take each day as it comes. We'll just follow our whims, enjoying the freedom to ramble. If we find a village or some little idyllic spot where we want to stay for a few days, that's where we'll stay. We don't have to worry about being a servant to an inflexible itinerary or to advance hotel reservations. If we have to end up sleeping in a hostel—or in our car—instead of a hotel, well, that isn't the end of the world. We've done it before as newlyweds, and we can certainly do it again.

Admittedly, not everyone would be comfortable with such a plan. Many people are completely hamstrung by fear of the unknown. But even people who need to know where they will lay their heads each night can reserve blocks of free time as the element of exchange for spontaneity and experience. Maybe you will plan out where you are going to stay but leave your days open for discovery. In any given area, the locals always know more about interesting experiences than the tour books do!

This same openness to new experiences works with little daily decisions, too. Just yesterday the kids invited some friends from school to attend our church's Thursday night prayer meeting with us.

"Great," I said. "Are we all going to go to dinner first?"

"Well," Nanette replied, "the kids were hoping we might grab a burger somewhere. Maybe a drive-through place."

"Wait a minute," I said. "There's a place I've been wanting to try—an old fifties-style hamburger stand on a side road near the church. What do you say we leave a few minutes early and give it a try?"

It turned out to be quite an event! Thursday night was "hot rod" night at the diner. While we were eating, people from all over the area kept pulling into the parking lot in wild hot rods and customized Harley Davidson bikes.

It was a spontaneous car show, and everybody had so much fun we were almost late to church. Before bed that night, I was reflecting on how such a little decision—a simple choice to do something out of the ordinary and off the beaten path—had turned out to be so fun and memorable for everyone. All it took was a little spontaneity, a little willingness to flex, and just a few extra dollars. But now we have a shared experience we'll always treasure, rather than one more generic and forgettable trip to a fast-food place.

That's a small example of what can happen over and over again in a marriage and a family as you step off the usual and expected course to risk a new direction.

I can anticipate some cynic replying, "But what if one of those variations doesn't turn out so well? What if you're in Europe and you find nowhere to stay one night? What if that fifties diner had turned out to be a greasy spoon with watery shakes and soggy fries?"

What if, indeed?

That's the way it works when you take a risk. Sometimes you find a tunnel through the mountain to a fairyland village on the other side, and sometimes you run smack into a mountainous dead end and have to listen to your friends say, "I told you so."

But here's something else that's true: Good or bad, you'll have an experience to talk about and laugh about around the kitchen table years from now. Someone will say, "Remember the night when…?" And you'll be reliving an adventure together instead of reciting your problems or rehearsing your aches and pains.

One thing for sure, you'll never get to Heiligenblut by staying eternally entrenched in your comfort zone.

ROLE MODELS

I've always been inspired by Nanette's father and mother. When I was just a boy, I loved to hang around their house and hear them tell stories about their exploits and adventures around the world. It was obvious that they loved each other very much, which was a wonderful thing for a boy from a single-parent home to see. And although they never had much money, they had a wealth of memories and experiences that seemed to bond them together as husband and wife.

By searching out opportunities to work in American schools overseas, Nanette's dad was able to give his family the world.

Nanette: 🌿

My dad is a lot like Thom. He's always loved adventure. He and Mom have planned a major move virtually every year of their lives. Before we moved to Placerville, we'd lived in both Japan and the Philippines. And every family vacation I can remember involved some sort of out-of-the-ordinary adventure—whether it was a boating expedition off the Alaskan coast or driving cross-country to Mexico for a fishing trip. It was always something different.

Dad's still like that. They're building a house right now, when many people their age are checking into retirement facilities. They've just returned from a three-year stint in Malaysia—loaded up with enough fresh stories to keep us all entertained for days on end.

Mom and Dad have been married for forty-

> *I've concluded that a rich, interesting life boils down to an attitude of the heart, not material circumstances.*

five years, and they will never, never lack for experiences to remember or things to talk about.

What I learned from them is that if you have a dream of experiencing new things, just pack up and find a way to do it. They never had any money to speak of, but always found a way. They never allowed the limitations of finances to stand in the way of living a full life or of sharing that adventure with the family. After watching the way they've lived through the years, I've concluded that a rich, interesting life boils down to an attitude of the heart, not material circumstances. ✻

THE STORY OF YOUR MARRIAGE is an artifact, a journal being written by two people. It is a reaction to the experience of living; it is a record of achievements and experiences, heartaches and triumphs. No one has any idea how many years of life God will grant, but whether that time be long or short, you can make the pages of your journal full and rich with exploration.

RISKING YIELDS NEWFOUND STRENGTH

Some people, of course, will live out their entire lives in a state of paralysis, constantly afraid to risk or venture into the unknown. I remember talking with a young couple who told me, "We would like to have children, but—we're not sure we could handle it. So we've decided against it."

I couldn't believe my ears. What a terrible criterion for making a decision! Who knows if you can "handle it"—or handle *anything*, for that matter—unless you try?

In retrospect, that was one of those conversations where I probably should have nodded my head and remained diplomatically silent. But I didn't.

"Life," I replied, "is far too short to avoid risks. What are you going to tell me next—that you're afraid to go on a hike because someone might turn an ankle? Or that you're afraid to plan a trip because you might get a flat tire somewhere? Or afraid to camp in a state park because a bear might break into your cooler?"

Keep living that way and you'll end up stuck on your couch at home, getting intravenous feedings of the experiences of others.

Sadly, more and more people are beginning to live just like that. In fact, I have some friends from years ago who adhere to this hollow philosophy. I will say, "What are you guys doing this summer? Where are you going on vacation?" And they will reply, "Oh, we're just staying home. We may rent a few movies. We've been tired—and, besides, we have some errands we've been needing to run."

What I have begun to see in many people is a fear of real experiences, and an addiction to the artificial, human-engineered "experiences" provided by the entertainment industry. Just listen to some of the conversations you hear around the watercooler at work. "Did you see such-and-such movie? Did you watch so-and-so's show last night? Wasn't that great?" Whatever happened to living life *yourself*, rather than second- or thirdhand? Real life will always contain an element of risk, an element of the unknown, an element of surprise about it. And if we don't reach for those shining opportunities, if we don't seek out such experiences, we will never taste the sweet serendipities that might have been ours. Living in an illusion of prudence and safety, we could put our marriage relationship in peril of a fatal disease.

Death by boredom.

Nanette: 🌿

We've all heard about people in middle age—especially men—who find themselves in a "midlife crisis." Somewhere along the line, they wake up to the fact that their life is half over, and feel trapped by their circumstances and choices. The simple fact for many of these men is that they've allowed themselves to become deeply entrenched in a constricting, colorless rut. They've become busy doing the same things over and over, so enslaved to the daily routines that they begin to despair of life ever changing. They begin to visualize their threescore-and-ten as just one boring day after another.

And so they rebel in some insane way, doing things that are illogical, out of character, and totally out of sync with who they really are and what they truly value and love. It's just a reaction to that gray, confining box—the feeling that life is closing in on them.

We've had some close Christian friends over the years—including some pastors—who became so caught up in their work, squeezed so dry by their responsibilities, that they wound up falling into affairs, destroying their families, destroying their very lives. Several of these incidents weren't only tragic; they were utterly absurd. We knew very well that these men loved their wives, loved their kids, loved their work and ministry. But they allowed themselves to become vulnerable to a lie from the adversary—seizing some short-lived and destructive escape from a box they should have never crawled into in the first place.

To me, that speaks of a couple that has allowed all of the adventure, fun, and spontaneity to leech out of their lives until there's nothing left but sameness and dryness and boredom.

There are so many simple little things that you can do to make your life and marriage more varied and interesting. Do something out of the ordinary now and then—something you've never done before. Shock some people who've known you for years. But make sure you do it *together*. Go on a cruise, or on a cross-country jaunt in a hot-air balloon. Take your bikes into the country and go on a picnic. Take a raft trip down the river. Enroll in a class together at the community college. Take tennis lessons. Go snowshoeing on a moonlit night. Take up in-line skating. Join a square-dance club.

Better still, find out about a short-term missions opportunity through your church or some Christian organization. Put yourself in a new culture for a season, and reach out together to meet some desperate needs.

There's no reason to fall into an affair if you're meeting each other's sexual and emotional needs and if you're cultivating a sense of purpose, adventure, and fun in your relationship.

THE HAPPY ACCIDENT

Your life together as a couple is a canvas, and your experiences are the brush. Someone might say to me, "Well, you speak glibly of being spontaneous. But surely, as a professional artist, you must follow a rather detailed plan of what you're going to paint when you approach the easel."

Not necessarily! There have been times I have sat down in front of a white canvas with a brush full of paint and simply plunged in because I had a vision dancing in my brain. Each new painting is a journey of discovery. You have to leave room for what I call the "happy accident"—those sudden flashes of inspiration that can change the whole character and direction of a painting.

> *Your life together as a couple is a canvas, and your experiences are the brush.*

One of my all-time heroes, Norman Rockwell, didn't allow much room for happy accidents in his art. Known for his meticulous preparation, he would plan every wrinkle and every freckle on every face in elaborate charcoal predrawings—the labor of many days. As Rockwell put it, "I don't want any surprises when I get to the painting phase. I want to know what everything is and where it goes." From there he would proceed to his color studies, preferring not to leave any aspect of color or mood or atmosphere for the final canvas.

Following all those pre-steps, he would move into the final painting phase—which became little more than an exercise in routine completion by that point. That was satisfying to him because it provided a safety net of comfort and security.

As much as I revere Rockwell, I have a very different approach. Just recently I was working on a lighthouse painting that began its life as a moonlit scene. I started with an idea of painting a lighthouse, up on a great rock, by moonlight—which is an unusual effect for me. The farther I got into the process, however, the more I struggled with a vague frustration. In my heart, I was tugged toward a luminous dusk, rather than moonlight.

I decided to follow my heart.

I began to lighten the values, adding a pinkish tone in the distance and highlights on the rocks and structures. Before I was done, I didn't have a lighthouse by moonlight, or even a lighthouse in a luminous dusk.

I had a radiant sunset, unlike anything I've painted before.

I also found myself with an incredible new palette, very different from my normal ranges, creating an effect that was both unusual and highly satisfying to me.

I call it "Rock of Salvation."

Looking back on that process, it's interesting to me that the foundations in my painting—the great rock and the lighthouse—never moved, never changed, through all of those variations. The color values, however, changed dramatically.

Maybe there's a lesson there about marriage. Change the things you can. Let a thousand colors come and go; savor hues in every variation. But hold firmly to those things that bring stability, salvation, and light when the fog rolls in and the night grows very dark.

Paint the lighthouse any shade you like, but build your marriage on the Rock.

Home.

It is your sanctuary,

your refuge, your

antidote to all

the world offers.

CHAPTER SEVEN

A Sheltering Love

W e had two little children and life was beginning to change.

As a young husband and father, I had begun to paint subjects that reflected my growing passion for tranquil, peaceful settings dancing with light.

But peace seemed hard to come by in those early days of the 1990s.

Nanette and I had moved back to Placerville from Los Angeles, hoping to perhaps recapture the simpler, less frenetic days of our youth. Someone once said that "you can't go home again." In one sense, it's true. Placerville had changed, and so had we. The stress of running a fledgling business was steadily tapping my creative energies—and that all-important time at the easel.

The need for peace and quiet had become like a physical hunger in our lives. We longed for it and began to think, *If we have to go halfway around the world to a little rustic cottage in an English village to find it, then that's what we'll do.*

And so we did just that.

ONCE UPON A TIME, IN A VILLAGE FAR, FAR AWAY...

As Nanette has already mentioned, Fairford is a walker's paradise. Kids walk to school. Families walk to church. Homemakers walk into the village every other day for groceries. Old-timers walk to the pub for an evening pint or two. And seemingly the whole town turns out at sunset to walk their dogs.

One evening I sat in the pub with a new friend

named John, a man in his sixties who had never in his life been more than thirty miles outside of Fairford. He had never even been to London, a little less than an hour away. He didn't own a car, but pedaled about the village every day on his rusty bicycle. John would probably never see the world...and it didn't seem to worry him a bit.

Life truly was simpler, and we relished it. There was a sense of small moments treasured, of relaxed conversations at the greengrocer's or bakery, of long evening rambles along cobbled roads and well-trod pathways.

Nanette and I, a couple of kids from California, couldn't get over how *old* everything was. As we looked at some of the historic homes and cottages on our evening strolls, we began to see them as monuments to families who had occupied them for generations.

In our country, something is considered old after fifty years, and if it's a hundred years old, it's a "historic landmark." In the past couple of years, cities like Seattle and Pittsburgh have imploded mammoth multimillion-dollar sports complexes that were built in the 1970s. Why? Because they were "too old."

One cottage we stayed in during our adventure in England was built in the 1100s. *Imagine.* People in

America talk about staying in a "historic inn" if it was built in 1935. Yet we frequently encountered dwellings that were a thousand years old or more. We were often assured that those smooth, worn boards beneath our feet were the original flooring. It's just a little bit awe-inspiring to think of treading across the same floor that families had been walking on for some four hundred years before Columbus set sail for the new world.

> *Life truly was simpler, and we relished it.*

England, of course, has its busy industrial cities, crowded highways, and congested suburbs. But out in the countryside, in the little towns and villages, you can't escape that sense of stepping back in time.

Nanette and I were impressed with Fairford's tolerant, respectful attitude toward everyone—even the eccentrics of the town.

I ought to know. I was one. As the "daft American artist," I was always treated with that slightly amused British cordiality; everyone greeted us and everyone wanted to talk to us.

Something happened to me that golden summer that to this day I find difficult to describe. I left that little English village ten years ago, but the village has never left me. The impression on my soul was permanent. The imprint on my artwork was incalculable. *Those venerable thatch-roofed cottages...the winding foot-paths through twilight pastures...the narrow cobblestone streets...the sleepy country gardens, with roses climbing the sun-warmed walls...the old stone bridges arching over languid summer streams...the little shops and inns and pubs with shining windows.* I was a changed man, and that's just what I wanted to be.

I told myself, "I'm not sure I can ever do it, but there's something here I want to capture with my paints. A peaceful village filled with light that says 'welcome' to one and all."

I've carried that desire with me ever since. But it's something more than a style of painting, something more than quaint, nostalgic landscapes with soft edges.

It's a way of life.

It's a promise of peace, laughter, and simpler times. Why should it exist only in a dream world? Why can't it be a picture of life today? God helping me, that's what I want for my marriage and my family.

THE REFUGE

Home. It is your sanctuary, your refuge, your antidote to all the world offers.

The world offers you noise...here's your place of quiet.

The world offers you hurry-up, speed-up, do-more... here's your place to slow down and relax.

The world offers you stress and pressure...here's your place to step out from under the load.

The world has its share of ugliness, crudity, cynicism, and exploitation...here's your place to find mutual respect, esteem, and love.

God gave us a home as a small retreat against the hurts and storms of life on a fallen planet. This identity of home should be central to who we are as Christians, and I do not take it lightly. Though I have never built a home in my life, I view myself as being in the "home business"—someone who enhances home environments, who creates small corners of refuge and sanctuary.

Nanette and I cherish that refuge. Within those protective, sheltering walls, we open our hearts and lives to one another. I don't hesitate to share with Nanette when I am going through something in our business or in my personal life, and she does the same with me. *What do you think about the kids' curriculum? What do you think about having people over for the Fourth of July? How did your checkup go? How did it go with Merritt's teacher this afternoon? Did you talk to your mom?* We talk our evenings away—and stay connected.

Nanette relies on that support, and we aim for decisions that blend her perspectives with mine. What a work of art God created when He ordained marriage! Just a few days ago, I was reading *The Message's* paraphrase of the book of Mark, and I came across a comment Jesus made to the Pharisees. He told them exactly how God felt about marriage—and about the destruction of that union through divorce:

> *"Moses wrote this command [allowing divorce] only as a concession to your hard-hearted ways. In the original creation, God made male and female to be together. Because of this, a man leaves father and mother, and in marriage he becomes one flesh with a woman—no longer two individuals, but forming a new unity. Because God created this organic unity of the two*

sexes, no one should desecrate his art by
cutting them apart."

MARK 10:5–9

That part about desecrating the art of God stopped this artist in his tracks. I had a mental picture of some magnificent Rembrandt being sliced down the middle with a box opener. Marriage *is* God's masterwork: infinitely balanced, exquisitely crafted, designed to benefit men, women, and children, and worthy of all the protection we can give it. Would you store a priceless painting in the garage behind the lawn mower and the kitty litter? Would you set your coffee mug down on an original Mozart score?

No, masterpieces deserve protection and great care.

And God's great masterpiece, man and woman joined in marriage, deserves all the care and shelter we can possibly provide. The home is the gallery where God has placed this work of art on display before the wondering eyes of men and angels.

SANCTUARY OR BATTLE ZONE?

You can use your home as a place of romance and a place of ritual that enhances your relationship. I love the idea that Nanette and I set up special places and corners in our home that call us into deeper companionship and romantic love.

Just recently, I went out and bought a small, inexpensive CD player that would fit in one little nook in our home. It was the one place in the house where we didn't have music.

We put a little collection of some of our favorite "soft music" CDs in the corner of this room, which also happens to contain a very important piece of Kinkade furniture: our snuggle couch. It is a big, heavy couch so deep and soft that you almost need help getting out of it. Here's a place where we can sit and cuddle, enjoy some romantic music, and let the pressures and worries of the day slip right off our shoulders.

What can the world offer us better than what we offer each other?

For so many of the people I talk to, home isn't a refuge at all; it's just another battle zone, full of noise, confusion, and even hostility.

The TV blares away in the living room, the phone rings incessantly, and laser blasts and planetary explosions erupt from a computer game down the hall.

Though you may not be able to control all of the factors that bring tension and confusion into your home environment, you can certainly control *those*. As I've mentioned, we don't include television in our home. From day one, the kids have found alternative, quieter ways to amuse themselves. As far as we can see, it hasn't warped their personalities at all. To the amazement and incredulity of their friends, they've discovered that the world of books and family activities holds endless excitement and enchantment.

Another simple thing we do is to keep our phone on "no ring" mode at night. When someone calls, the answering machine automatically answers. As a result, we don't have to share our mealtimes or precious family moments with those seeking to drop in unannounced via telephone. Our kids' friends know this and have learned to make all their arrangements and contacts during the day. We've made it very evident to friends, extended family, and business associates that we simply don't take calls at night. Period. If it isn't life or death, it can wait until the next day.

Just eliminating those two sources of noise and confusion—the phone and the TV—makes a monumental difference.

It's quiet.

It's peaceful.

You can hear laughter and chatter through the walls.

There's time for family fun without distraction and—after the kids head for bed—adult conversations and quiet moments.

Withdrawing from the world, you say? Becoming insulated and exclusive, you frown? *Yes.* And why not? Why not savor our own little world of kindness, beauty, laughter, light, and love? Why conform to arbitrary cultural norms that steal our time and quench our joy? What can the world offer us better than what we offer each other?

The tyranny of the urgent, the pressure of a thousand demands from numberless sources, simply overpowers the simplicity of truly important things. So we have made some choices—not as radical as they might seem on the surface—to shelter and protect our marriage and home life.

And we've never regretted it.

We're one of those rarities in the twenty-first century…a happily married couple.

WHEN LIFE IMITATES ART

Many of those who buy my paintings are drawn to the affirmation of home portrayed there. The lights are on, and smoke curls from the chimney. You can almost smell the cookies in the oven or hear the logs crackling and popping in the fireplace. *Someone is home*, and you are invited in. People who collect my work view the paintings as something good and positive they can do for their own homes—and aspire to the worlds created in those painted scenes. When people tell me that they want to *live* in one of my paintings, I think it's something more than wistful dreaming or escapism. I believe that these good people truly want to bring some of those qualities of peacefulness and simplicity into lives that have become too complicated and loaded with stress. What they are really saying is, "I want my real life to be more like the world I see in this painting."

Nanette: ❧

Those cozy homes and country lanes in Thom's paintings are universal symbols for family, warmth, and security. He loves evoking those feelings—that sense of well-being and of all things being "right with the world."

People seek to project themselves into the paintings because the paintings present places of peace and comfort. We're reminded of happy experiences and quiet moments in our past. People have told us time and again that spending a few moments with one of Thom's paintings is like a "sanity break" in the day. It gives them a chance to step out of a more busy, complicated, harried experience and take a little minivacation into a quiet, restful place.

This pleases Thom to no end. Nothing excites and motivates him more than when someone says, "With all my heart, I just want to walk down that little path and sit on that bench in that garden." It is deeply fulfilling to him when someone tells him how he or she has entered the world of one of his paintings and experienced feelings of rest and well-being.

That's exactly what Thom is trying to share when he paints his images. He wants to bring people into a place of peace and, more importantly, closer to the Prince of Peace.

Even those of us who have been Christians for many years sometimes forget to take those few minutes now and then to push back from our work, take a deep breath, ponder the Lord who loves us, and allow ourselves to be drawn back to Reality. And what is Reality?

> *God is our refuge and strength,*
> *   an ever present help in trouble.*
> *Therefore we will not fear, though*
> *   the earth give way*
> *   and the mountains fall into*
> *   the heart of the sea,*
> *though its waters roar and foam*
> *   and the mountains quake with*
> *   their surging.*

PSALM 46:1–3

Reality tells us that our God is always with us and that His strength is eminently available to those who call upon Him...*no matter what.* Most of the churning activity and freneticism that disturbs us and causes us such worry and tension is just on the surface of things. Deep down, below those surface waves and spray and froth, God's love and plans for our lives have not changed. 🐾

SHAME AND LONGING

When I was a boy, I used to love visiting my Placerville pals, spending my time in their homes and playing in their driveways, bedrooms, or backyards. But they all knew that there was one thing they would rarely receive from Thom Kinkade.

A return invitation.

I didn't want anyone to see my home.

I grew up in a small, shabby single-parent home at the end of a long dirt driveway. Our yard was knee-high with weeds and wild grass, and when my brother, Pat, and I came home from school at night, the windows were often dark. With Mom sometimes working a long shift at the office, there was often no one home when we returned in the evening.

Embarrassed by the appearance of our home, Pat and I developed a few survival habits. When someone gave us a ride from somewhere, we'd never let them turn in to our driveway. We would always say, "Oh, just drop us off here, out on the road. Our house is down at the end of a dinky dirt road, and, well, you just can't turn around down there."

Pat and I laugh about that, looking back. It was hugely important to us that no one see our run-down environment. If they tried to be nice and insist on taking us to the front door, we'd get just a little more determined. "You'd better not try it," we would insist. "It's almost *impossible* to turn around! You might get blocked in!"

As a child and young man, I not only missed having a dad; I craved the identity of a normal home. My mom did her best with the time and financial means at her disposal, but I still longed for something that was an expression of excellence and pleasing to the eye.

More than anything, in an era when divorce was unusual, I longed to have a home life like other kids around me. With Mom working every moment to put clothes on our backs and food on the table, and with us kids doing our best to keep up with school and social activities, the home environment invariably suffered.

Even though we were out in the country a bit, we did have neighbors who had time to keep their houses up to suburban standards.

I still chuckle when I remember our next-door neighbor, a very particular elderly gentleman who would slowly creep down his long driveway in a grand, silver Cadillac—big as a battleship—with a fat cigar clamped between his teeth. Kind, tolerant, and crowned with immaculately trimmed silver hair, my neighbor represented the rural gentry of Placerville.

With the abundant hours available in his retirement, this man was a fanatic about his lawn. If one little blade of crabgrass dared to raise its humble head upon his turf, the lord of the manor was out of the house in a heartbeat, rooting it out with a tiny spade and barely suppressed fury.

> *I not only missed having a dad; I craved the identity of a normal home.*

Of course, being next door to a well-kept home with a putting-green lawn and magazine-perfect flowerbeds made our poor old place look even more shabby and neglected by comparison.

Since those days, both Pat and I have been relatively successful in life, and each of us has a comfortable home of his own. It's the fulfillment of a lifelong dream and longing: Each of us has that special place of refuge, bright and welcoming, that can be shared with others. Somehow, I don't think either of us will ever take it for granted.

SWEET SHELTER

Part of the way Nanette and I shelter our home is simply by sheltering each other. By emotionally affirming and esteeming each another, we help each other work through personal weaknesses.

Nanette depends on me for that. By loving and treasuring her, by creating surprises and weaving memories with her, I help her to deal with the frustrations and weaknesses that might otherwise cause her unhappiness and a loss of confidence.

At the same time, she's also doing that for me. We have both depended on that teamwork for the last two decades. In fact, it just keeps getting better.

Nanette: 🌿

*P*art of what it means to have a sheltering love is to overlook and cover for each other in our areas of weakness.

Where one is weak, the other is strong. When one is discouraged, the other steps in with a smile and a positive word. We're there for each other through all the highs and lows.

It's been an ongoing source of kidding within the Kinkade home that Mom is "directionally challenged." For some reason, I seem to be quite inept about directions, and I have to ask Thom to draw me a map any time I venture into an unfamiliar area. The directions that seem like second nature to so many people just don't compute in my brain. I get completely boggled and have to have a map—or I'm in trouble!

Sometimes I feel embarrassed to ask Thom for a map to someplace nearby. I keep telling myself, *I should know how to do this!* But for whatever reason, I just can't figure it out.

Now, that could make great fodder for jokes with other couples or at parties. Thom could make a big deal about this blond lady who is clueless about directions. It would be an easy way to get laughs.

But he doesn't do that. He doesn't demean me or make me feel incompetent or foolish. He understands that I need some covering in this area, and he consistently helps me without making me feel strange about it.

That may sound like something small or insignificant, but it means so much to me. He is sympathetic of my needs, protective of my self-esteem, and always willing to help. He protects me and helps me in an area where I truly feel weak and vulnerable.

A sheltering love moves in to assist and encourage, rather than criticize, nag, or ridicule.

I try to do the same for him with his weaknesses. I may not be as creative as Thom, but he would be the first to admit that I'm more organized, and he can rely on my orderly, analytical approach to things when he's feeling harried. That kind of support is really important to him, and frees him up to do what I believe he does better than anyone else in the world: create inspiring visions on canvas of tranquil places.

Thom works extremely hard at his painting and doesn't pay much attention to the condition of his studio. After a while, it all starts to stack up around him—the scraps of paper, the books, the tapes, the sketches, the painting supplies. He claims it's a geyser that periodically spews debris from behind his easel and he can't figure out where it's all coming from.

It would be terribly distracting for Thom if he had to stop a couple of times a day to reorganize his environment. He would find himself spending less and less time at his easel.

For me, the orderliness comes much easier. It's one of my strengths. I can dive into the geyser and put things back in order in a short amount of time, without interrupting his creative flow. He's so grateful for that help. Again, it may not seem like a great matter, but the relief and gratitude that wells up in Thom's heart is very important to me as his wife. That's his vulnerable area, and I like to "cover" him in this weakness so that he won't be uncomfortable or self-conscious if someone comes to visit him in his studio.

Unfortunately, mutual support is not always the order of the day. We've all seen how some couples seem to delight in humiliating one another in public, or try to get a cheap laugh at their spouse's expense. As husband and wife, of course, we have inside information. We know things about our spouse that others don't know. It's the same thing as parents. We know our children's weaknesses and where they are struggling. A sheltering love is very, very careful about ever exposing the weaknesses or struggles of a family member to ridicule. Knowing that Thom will never do that to me or the girls is just one more way that I depend on him.

And that kind of dependency strengthens the bonds of a marriage. A sheltering love moves in to assist and encourage, rather than criticize, nag, or ridicule.

THE SOURCE OF OUR STRENGTH

If you know anything about our life, ministry, and business, you would think that Nanette and I might face some rather extraordinary challenges.

And you would be right. We certainly do.

These days we find ourselves at the hub of an amazingly large and demanding organization, faced with commitments and deadlines that seem nothing less than ridiculous at times. Just the other day, I was reflecting on what a luxury it seems when I get to do "one thing at a time." It seems as though I always have to do two things at once: talk to business contacts on my telephone headset while I'm painting; sign prints while I'm giving an interview.

In spite of those pressures, I try to maintain a joyful attitude and have had to deeply depend on the Lord. Though I am often painfully aware of my own failings and frequent mistakes, I have learned to simply immerse myself in God. I don't know that anybody else worships Him in quite the peculiar way I do—not that my form of devotion is any more special than anyone else's! I take time with God, praying to Him, praising Him, and worshiping Him with my paintbrush, at times even dancing a jig of joyful celebration in my studio. In times of extreme need, I might even lay prostrate on my office rug, clinging like a child to His garments.

In short, I depend on Him all day long, and so does Nanette. Although the pressure becomes very intense at times, we just face it one day at a time, asking the Lord for enough strength to meet the demands of that day, that hour, that minute.

And He faithfully meets those needs.

We are partners with God in this life. And I don't shy away at all from the image of our marriage and home as a fortress under attack, under siege. Let's face it, life on this broken, fallen planet *is* a battle much of the time.

It's you and your spouse against the pressures and challenges of life.

It's you and your spouse against the attacks of our spiritual enemy.

It's you and your spouse against a culture in free fall.

It's you and your spouse against the people who would wound you, bring you down, or seek to harm you.

It's you and your spouse against the stresses and difficulties and trials.

God never intended us to fight life's battles alone. In marriage, He gave us one another. And through it all, He reminds us that He is our ultimate strength, wisdom, and defense against all that life might throw against us. After all, *The battle is the Lord's!*

*Our life
purpose is to be
radiant lights
within a dark and
unhappy world.*

CHAPTER EIGHT

A Beacon of Love

O ne way or another, my buddy Jim Gurney and I promised ourselves we would see America from coast-to-coast that summer.

And when our hitchhiking, rail-riding hobo odyssey finally brought us to the very tip of Cape Cod on the Atlantic seaboard, we knew we'd arrived. We felt about as far from California as we could possibly be.

After hitching a ride into Provincetown, Massachusetts, on a cool, misty evening, we hiked down to the bay shore to see what we might see. Out on a small point, an old stone lighthouse seemed to rise out of the mist, towering over us like some primordial creature coming out of the sea.

It was an eerie experience, looking up at that tall structure as the mist curled in off the bay. As we walked up to the door, Jim turned to me. "What should we do?" he asked.

"Let's just knock on the door," I said, "and see if anyone's home."

"Oh, come on! Do people still *live* in these places? I thought it was all automated these days."

"I guess we'll find out," I said and knocked loudly on the stout wooden door.

After a minute or two, we distinctly heard the sound of footsteps descending the long spiral staircase. With the click of a rusty deadbolt, the door creaked open...and the hair stood up on the backs of our necks.

Who was this? The resident lighthouse ghost?

The man who opened the door looked like he'd just stepped out of a Winslow Homer painting. Jim and I glanced at each other, not believing our eyes. We found ourselves looking into the craggy face of an old seaman—with a captain's cap on his head and a long sou'wester cloaking his lanky body. All he was missing was the beard and the pipe.

Truthfully, the lighthouse keeper seemed just as surprised to see us as we were to encounter him. Apparently there weren't many people who walked right up and knocked on his door on a foggy, pitch-black night.

We explained that we were artists traveling across the country, and after exchanging a few light comments, he invited us in for coffee. After we got acquainted a bit, he consented to sitting for a portrait. Jim and I hastily pulled sketchbooks out of our backpacks and began penciling the tranquil, weathered features, hardly believing our luck.

ISLAND OF LIGHT

Mysterious and magnetic, lighthouses hold an endless fascination for me.

They're beautiful, yes. But just a little bit eerie, too.

When you stop to think about it, when does a lighthouse come alive? In night and gloom. In storm and fog. In shrieking gale and shrouding mist. Yet if you found yourself lost on a dark sea, sailing near the rocks, what could be more comforting than that stab of radiance from an invisible shore?

When I was a young boy, I visited San Francisco for the first time with my father. Who would have thought that summer in California could be so damp and cold? Mark Twain was said to have remarked, "The coldest winter I ever saw was the summer I spent in San Francisco." Even so, it wasn't the cold that gave me chills as much as the deep, spine-tingling bellows of the foghorns from the buoys and lighthouses along the bay. (These days, the foghorns have been emasculated; they've gone from basso profundo to a piping soprano.)

> *Mysterious and magnetic, lighthouses hold an endless fascination for me.*

What a sensation those lighthouses created in my imagination! For months and even years afterward, I would fantasize about a great sea of darkness and a little beacon rising up in the middle of it...like an island of light, pushing back the gloom and night.

It wasn't until 1994 that I considered using a lighthouse as an element in one of my paintings for publication. When I first told our company's directors my plans to paint a "romantic lighthouse scene," the response was something less than overwhelming. In fact, they became just a tad anxious.

"Umm…are you sure we can sell prints of this, Thom?"

Sometimes my business associates seem to forget that I'm an artist and that when I paint something it is because I have a *passion* to paint it and believe God can use it. And I had a vision in my mind that I couldn't wait to commit to canvas.

I saw high waves breaking over the rocks. I saw a pale evening sky, the fleeing storm clouds tinged with rose. I saw a lighthouse and, alongside, a little, gray, stone keeper's house with a bay window and a red roof. I saw the welcoming light from its windows reflecting off the sea-drenched rocks in the gathering twilight.

My colleagues worried in vain. "Beacon of Hope" became one of our all-time bestselling prints—and I returned to the lighthouse motif again and again in the years that followed.

With some of my collectors, it's become the favorite theme of all.

Nanette: ❧

Thom has always loved lighthouses for their aesthetic beauty, but more important for their symbolism of God's light in our lives. The lighthouse is a point of luminance in the dark and storm, giving lifesaving direction and guidance. That comparison, especially, is what keeps drawing Thom to that image in his paintings.

Historically, lighthouses were also homes, inhabited by whole families. A home is such a reflection of who we are, and when we see a lighthouse attached to a home, it reminds us of the impact a Christian marriage can have on our culture. Here's hope in the darkest and stormiest of times!

"The Light of Peace" is one of my favorite lighthouse paintings. It's loosely based on a view near our cottage in Carmel, California. It is a powerful, picturesque piece, and it draws me all the more because of the familiar setting. It's a place where we've walked and played together as a family.

On a recent trip to a large showing of Thom's work in the Midwest, one of our collectors handed Thom a photo of his backyard...and what he had constructed there. Stone by stone, the man had lovingly erected a towering lighthouse in his backyard, complete with a rotating beacon at the top. He had built it over the course of many months, in honor of one of Thom's lighthouse paintings. He's such a supercollector that he wanted a Kinkade lighthouse of his very own! Even so, I can't help wondering how his neighbors feel about a fully operational lighthouse in the middle of a midwestern subdivision. ❀

I CAN'T IMAGINE A MORE potent symbol of the life purpose of believers, our life purpose as radiant lights within a dark and unhappy world. A lighthouse structure may be delightful and pleasing in itself, but it actually has only one purpose: to save lives. Its strong beacon sweeping across the waters is both a comforting guide and a stern warning. Heed the light and you'll find safe harbor. Ignore it and you may lose yourself and all you care about on the unforgiving rocks.

What's even more fascinating to me is that the lighthouses up and down our coasts are not only towers of hope, help, and warning for the storm-tossed; each is also somebody's home. Though it may not always be so today, someone at one time lived in these outposts—a lighthouse keeper and his family.

Mom crocheted in her favorite chair, Dad played checkers with his son, and two little daughters put their dolls to bed while scant yards from their living area a great and piercing beacon of light sent out a strong beam of hope, help, and deliverance.

In *The Message*'s paraphrase of the Sermon on the Mount, Jesus told His disciples:

> *"You're here to be light, bringing out the God-colors in the world. God is not a secret to be kept. We're going public with this, as public as a city on a hill. If I make you light-bearers, you don't think I'm going to hide you under a bucket, do you? I'm putting you on a light stand. Now that I've put you there on a hill-top, on a light stand—shine! Keep open house; be generous with your lives. By opening*

up to others, you'll prompt people to open up with God, this generous Father in heaven."

MATTHEW 5:14–16

As an artist, I love that visual image. A city on a hill...light streaming out into the night, visible for miles and miles. Imagine such a city in Jesus' day. Where would that light be coming from? There were no streetlights, car headlights, traffic lights, or flashing neon signs. No, the light came from individual homes—homes lit from within by tiny oil lamps shining through open windows.

> *Even the smallest of lights can be seen from miles away in the darkness.*

Even the smallest of lights can be seen from miles away in the darkness. I knew a man in Portland, Oregon, who would drive home at night over the Interstate Bridge, crossing the wide Columbia River. From a certain place on the bridge, he could look to the south and see the dark bulk of Rocky Butte—a towering hill in the city, some five miles away. And about halfway up on the shoulder of the butte, he could see his own tiny porch light—a twinkling diamond against the black velvet of night. But what drawing power that single little seventy-five-watt lightbulb had! It represented his wife, his children, his home, and all that he loved. He would always want to drive a little faster after seeing that pinpoint of light across the dark water.

The lights of home awaken longings deep within us. And when our homes and marriages are filled with joy and love, esteem and care, affection and conversation, an unhappy, cynical world just can't help noticing.

HOMETOWN LIGHTHOUSE

Nanette and I want our marriage and home to be a lighthouse on a hill, a beacon of hope in a contemporary world and culture that seems to grow darker and more hopeless by the day. I recently heard a statistic that over half of the homes in our country today are single-parent homes. Just twenty years ago, I remember that figure being closer to 15 percent.

When I was a boy in Placerville, divorce was almost unheard-of. It was like death by lightning bolt—something unusual and strange. I knew of only one other schoolmate whose parents had divorced. All my friends had dads at home, which made the ache of missing a father go even deeper.

When I speak to groups around the country about my love for my wife, it's like water in the desert for so many people in the audience. For many, a happy marriage seems like a distant dream.

I always tell my audience that though there's no such thing as a perfect marriage (mine included), I do think it's possible to have a "happy marriage." But whether or not an individual has been able to live out a dream of a happy marriage does not invalidate the dream itself. The vision is precious and the goal is priceless.

Granted, the goal isn't easy to attain. It takes a miraculous work of God to blend two lives into one harmonious whole. But the good news is that God is still available, and miracles do still happen. Nanette and I plan on staying dependent on God's hand of blessing for the rest of our lives.

Nanette: 🖎

One of the reasons Thom and I want our lives to be a light for others is because of a lighthouse marriage we encountered early in our relationship, back in our hometown.

Our friends had four children, but there was always room at their table for a young couple named Thom and Nanette. We were still dating at the time and found ourselves drawn to this family's home like moths to a bright porch light. It was such a warm, hospitable place. No matter what time of the day or night you dropped in, you always felt welcome.

We had Bible studies, we had times of prayer and praise, and sometimes we just needed to talk. When I think of a home being a lighthouse today, I think of the stability, the consistency, and the nonjudgmental acceptance of that couple in Placerville. The wife was such an example to me of a virtuous woman who had her priorities straight but never seemed "too busy" to be available.

Our relationship came full circle a few years ago, when one of the daughters in the family came into our home for a time as a live-in nanny for our girls. 🌼

EVEN THOUGH THIS FAMILY faced challenges and difficulties of their own, they always seemed to keep an outward focus—reaching out to those in need and even taking street people into their home on occasion.

No matter what they were going through—and some of their problems were hurtful and deep—they walked by faith, prayed constantly, had a lot of fun as a family, and never gave in to doubts or discouragement. They fought the good fight every day and made a deep impact on Nanette and me.

Thinking back on those dear friends, it's a reminder to us that while we cherish and treasure our close family times, we can't allow our focus to become introverted. Can you picture a lighthouse with closed blinds? Can you imagine a lighthouse keeper somehow focusing the powerful beam of that lighthouse down into the structure itself, instead of out across the water? What folly that would be! Though his own family might be bathed in radiance, those in ships out on the dark horizon would despair, possibly sailing straight into destruction.

In the same sense, a truly vital marriage needs to reach outside the confines of the Christian subculture or your own tight family circle.

Isn't that what being a city on a hill is all about?

THE "ODD COUPLE"

We have two important reasons for working out at a gym near our home…and the second one is to stay in shape. The most important reason is to stay in contact with those who need the Lord in their lives. Through much of an average week, Nanette and I find ourselves insulated in a comfortable Christian cocoon, surrounded by friends and family and colleagues who know and love God. The people in our church, for instance, have a high level of commitment. Most of them really love Jesus Christ and have a passion to serve Him.

Here's a couple that has been married for "eons" and love each other more than ever.

At the gym, it's a different story.

One trainer might be struggling with depression or drug addiction. Another might be living with his girlfriend and experiencing all kinds of stress and tension in the relationship. Because Nanette and I work out together and are so obviously in love with one another, we've become heroes to those twentysomething trainers. Every time we come in, they fight over who gets to work with us. Why?

Because they want to watch us interact.

They want to hear us talk about our marriage.

The fact that we've been happily wed for twenty years and intend to go the distance makes us something of a cultural curiosity.

As I try to bench-press some new, heavier weight, I'll groan aloud, "Where's Nanette? She's my inspiration. Let me look at her or I'll never get this bar off my chest!"

The trainers really have a hard time believing we're for real. Here's a couple that has been married for "eons" and love each other more than ever. After all those years and four kids, here are a husband and wife who hate to be apart and who talk to each other like high school sweethearts. The staff thinks it's hilarious...but they can't stop asking us questions and seeking our counsel.

It boils down to putting your life out there where people can see it—not as an example of pious perfection, but simply to say, "Despite our imperfections, God is central in our lives. Because of that, we experience help and hope every day."

When you think about it, there aren't that many examples of truly happy marriages out there. What do you see in movies and on television? Most likely, cynicism and betrayal. A stable, honoring, fun-loving marriage is portrayed as a relic of some bygone, mostly mythical, Ozzie and Harriett era. Oh, sure, the facades are out there—the politicians and celebrities who put on happy faces for the camera but then end up in some tabloid photo spread caught in an illicit affair. But what about the genuine article? What about the marriage that radiates joy and fun and commitment ten, twenty, or thirty years after the honeymoon?

You really could use that old "lost at sea" metaphor for today's cultural attitudes toward love and marriage. So many young couples have no baseline, no standards, no role models—and really, no clues—that show them how to achieve success in a marriage and in a family. Most people outside of a relationship with Christ are just trying to make it up as they go along, hoping against hope that their marriage won't end up on the beach with all those other shipwrecks. It may be a fragile, somewhat forlorn hope, but it's all they have.

Nanette and I have found that people are truly hungry to hear someone say, "Here's how we live. Here's how we've been successful. Here's how we've stayed in love and stayed faithful to one another through a thousand ups and downs."

For a number of years now, we have developed what

we call our "dinner ministry." It's very simple. We take people out to dinner and just talk about our lives and our Lord. We're not judgmental or condemning; we love all kinds of people (in all kinds of trouble and difficulty). It may be a couple struggling in their marriage, or even someone in the middle of an affair. We might invite a coworker battling financial difficulties, or just someone in need of a little friendship and encouragement.

It's not a dramatic, high-profile ministry, but it keeps us from becoming ingrown, self-satisfied, or stale in our own walk with Christ. We have found that reaching out to others—praying for them, sharing their loads, and lifting them up—helps as a couple to rebuild our own sense of dependency on God. And the fact that we do this together is yet another bridge that links our lives...and gives us one more way to learn and grow as a couple.

> *We take people out to dinner and just talk about our lives and our Lord.*

HOPE IN THE STORM

Earlier in the book, I mentioned those times when I've felt inspiration flow through me in the midst of a painting. That's just what happened to me as I began creating another lighthouse scene back in 1997. I called it "Clearing Storms," and from the first strokes of my brush, I felt God's presence and direction. I had an inexplicable, unshakable sense that He was going to use that painting in people's lives.

In fact, that's just what He has done.

A month or so after the print was released, a family approached me at one of our collectors' gatherings.

"Do you remember the recent hurricane?" they asked me.

I did remember reading about that storm. It had slammed into the Gulf Coast in July of that year and had been the most devastating hurricane in what meteorologists had called "a weak hurricane year."

The family standing in front of me, however, would have never used the term *weak* to describe their horrific encounter with the monster storm.

As it turned out, they had just purchased a print of "Clearing Storms," but they hardly had time to enjoy it before word came to evacuate their home.

After serious prayer and consideration, however, this family decided to ride it out, trusting the Lord to protect them and lead them through it. As the hurricane thundered in from the sea, they huddled together in a safe place in the house and began to pray. Someone in the family had the idea of bringing my painting in and setting it up on a table.

They gathered around it and prayed, "Lord, we just trust You that You are going to help us endure this long night and that—as this painting shows—the storm will clear."

Gradually, as daylight approached, the frightening winds subsided. When everyone went out the next day to check for damage, they couldn't find any. Even though trees had fallen all around them, they hadn't lost so much as a shingle.

The lady took pictures of her house after that storm and has used the story dozens of a times as a testimony of God's grace. "That lighthouse painting," she said, "gave us an extra measure of faith when we needed it."

That's the way it is with lighthouses—or even a painting of a lighthouse. If you can see that pinpoint of light, you can make it through, you can push back despair, you can find your way. Without that light, and with darkness pressing in all around, what hope can there be?

A strong, loving marriage can be that point of

light. A home where Jesus is Lord can be a city on a hill, drawing those who have traveled for countless miles in darkness.

It isn't that the skies over your home are always pastel blue, or that no storms or heavy circumstances ever stain your horizons. In fact, it is in the midst of those very storms that the light shines brightest. If your neighbors and family and friends can see you clinging to the Rock with all your might, they might come looking for that Refuge when their own storms descend.

Nanette: 🌿

So many people have written to Thom to tell him about how his art has touched their lives. One letter will talk about how one of his paintings eased the pain of losing a loved one. Someone else will tell him how a particular picture gave hope or strength or perseverance to make it through a time of deep turmoil or pain.

It's deeply satisfying to Thom to know that something God has enabled him to create has been a light post—or a lighthouse—in someone's life.

I know that even though I may never have that kind of life impact on people through what I might paint or write or create with my own hands, I still have the opportunity to let our marriage and home be that lighthouse.

The light we hold up for viewing, after all, isn't our own light at all. It's the light of God's Son. And the more we allow Him to work in our lives—broken and humble and insignificant as we may seem in our own eyes—the farther that light will reach into the darkness.

Our world needs lighthouse keepers more than ever. ✿

*Who knows
what loves await to
be discovered along
the golden pathways
of heaven?*

Two for the Road

P icture two backpackers, a man and a woman, setting out on a journey. As well as they are able, they
have prepared themselves for the long trek. They're excited.
They're also inexperienced, untested, unproven, and just a
little bit scared. Yet they have the essentials. They have a good
compass. They have provision. And they have each other.

The problem is, they have no idea at all where their

path will lead. They have a vague notion that there will be long climbs, beautiful vistas, deep canyons, long desert stretches, and swift rivers. Although bright sunlight will occasionally warm their shoulders, they also sense (however dimly) that rain will follow, the wind will blow, and snow may cover the trail.

At the same time, they can also appreciate the fact that each of them will change on this journey—as surely as the terrain transforms beneath their feet. Dark nights, heavy loads, long winds, and the heat of the day have a way of shaping a man or woman's soul. They will begin to see things through new eyes. They will find a pace that suits them both. They will adjust to weaknesses—whether of bone and sinew, or of the heart. They will develop attitudes and attributes significantly different from the way they viewed things at the trailhead.

But as the miles fall behind and the months and years slip by, they will continue to walk side by side. Sometimes helping each other across streams or up steep, rocky inclines, they maintain their long journey…into the unknown.

The landscape alters dramatically. Storms rage and pass on. Wildflowers bloom and wither. Seasons pass.

Companions on the trail come and go. And the hikers themselves adjust and grow through each experience, each amazing vista, each encounter with hardship and danger.

And they stay together.

Step for step. Day by day. Year after year. Their companionship is a constant as everything else changes. When one stumbles, the other is quick with a helping hand. When one becomes weary, the other shoulders two loads for a few miles. They weather the storms. They take shelter in each other's arms. They experience high country panoramas when life unfolds before them, shining like a rain-washed highway in the morning sun. Nothing, but nothing, drives them apart. Nothing short of death divides their path.

They are husband and wife.

Two against the world.

Two for the road, no matter where that road may lead.

The first leg of the journey is not like the third or fourth. The middle is not like the end. The first kiss is not like the ten thousandth. The first honeymoon is not like the second, twenty years later, or the third, twenty years after that. And who is to say which is the sweeter?

Expectations change. Circumstances change. Visions change. Personal identities change. Nanette and I were poor when we exchanged our vows in that little white church in the hills. Now we are experiencing career success and the blessing of financial resources. We were kids when we stepped into married life together. Beyond a little circle of friends and family, no one knew who we were—or cared. Now our names are known by many. We only had each other back in those early days of poverty and laughter in Los Angeles. Now there are six of us...five delightful females and one very blessed—and at times overwhelmed—husband and father.

We had the Lord at the beginning, and we have Him now, faithful and strong, forgiving and kind, providing for our every need.

We had a wild, romantic love at the beginning, and, though we've fought hard to maintain that love, we've discovered other loves worth celebrating.

An enduring love...that rides the rolling waves like a sailboat, drawing strength from the shifting winds.

An exploring love...that keeps us holding hands with excitement and a sense of adventure as we anticipate the next bend in the road.

An attentive love…that reminds us that the life we desire together is fragile and needs sunlight, water, and daily care.

A sharing love…in which we've seen that the view from the bridge between us is a wider, grander sight than we could have ever seen from either shore.

A spontaneous love…that embraces each new day with wide-open eyes and refuses to allow the pale and diminished expectations of others to dilute our joy.

A sheltering love…that protects our investment in one another from all that would erode its commitment or quench its flame.

A beacon of love…that unites us in a life purpose bigger than ourselves, bigger than our marriage, bigger than the whole world.

And beyond these, we've discovered a playful love, a familiar love, a serious love, a ravishing love, a spiritual love, a tender love, a merciful love, a contented love, and—how many others?

We won't know that until the end of the journey.

Did I say the end? For those who belong to Jesus Christ, *end* is just another word for the beginning of everything. Who knows what loves await to be discovered along the golden pathways of heaven?

With Nanette beside me, I can't wait to find out.

"THE PLEASURES OF PARENTAL LOVE ARE MANY,"

...say Thomas and Nanette Kinkade, who find that the "kaleidoscope" of life with their four daughters shifts colors day by day.

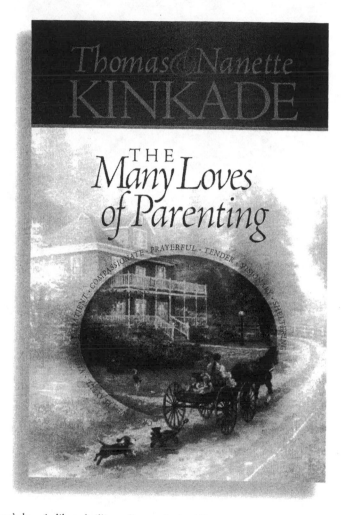

A parent's love is like a brilliant diamond, shedding its light on a child in countless ways—and who better to write about it than Thomas Kinkade, the beloved "Painter of Light™", and his wife Nanette? Their own experience with four daughters has taught them how a parent's love can take many forms: vigilant, focused, creative, compassionate, tough, playful, visionary, and releasing. Through every beautiful scene the couple illustrates our ultimate goal—a love like our heavenly Father's, giving us the ability and the will to love our children as He has loved us.

ISBN 1-59052-088-2

PAINTER OF LIGHT™ EXPLORES SEASON OF LIGHTS

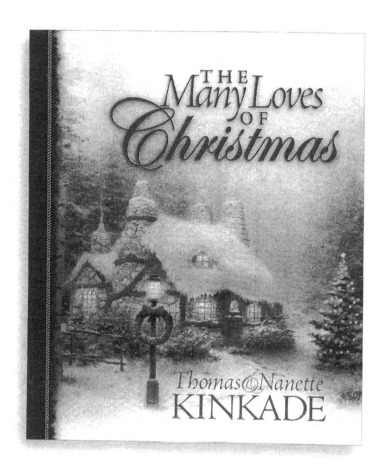

Beneath the commercialism of a season our culture now calls "the holidays," true Christmas waits to be rediscovered. It isn't about self-indulgence or shallow "good cheer" that evaporates on December 26. It's about love and giving. Those who celebrate true Christmas reflect this spirit. They are drawn to love cold winter, total strangers, friends and neighbors, family...and the Christ child Himself. Thomas and Nanette Kinkade share their thoughts, memories, and dreams in a book that honors the newborn King.

ISBN 1-59052-090-4

Printed in the United States
by Baker & Taylor Publisher Services